Our Lady of the Most Blessed Sacrament

READINGS FOR
THE MONTH OF MAY

FROM THE NOTES OF
Blessed Peter Julian Eymard

A new translation from the ninth French edition

THE SENTINEL PRESS
194 EAST 76TH STREET
NEW YORK 21. N. Y.

Nihil Obstat:

>EUGENIUS COUET,
>*Sup. Gen.*
>*Congr. S. S. Sacramenti.*

Roma 31ª Martii 1930.

Nihil Obstat:

>ARTHUR J. SCANLAN, S.T.D.,
>*Censor Librorum.*

Imprimatur:

>✠ PATRICK CARDINAL HAYES,
>*Archbishop of New York.*

New York, March 14, 1930.

CONTENTS

	PAGE
Foreword	v
Preparatory Meditation—The Month of Our Lady of the Most Blessed Sacrament	1
First Day—Mary, Mother of Eucharistic Adorers	10
Second Day—The Immaculate Conception and Holy Communion	16
Third Day—The Dowry of Mary Immaculate	22
Fourth Day—The Nativity of the Blessed Virgin	28
Fifth Day—Mary's Presentation in the Temple	32
Sixth Day—The Annunciation	38
Seventh Day—The First Adorer of the Incarnate Word	45
Eighth Day—The Dignity of the Divine Maternity	49
Ninth Day—The Interior Life of Mary	54
Tenth Day—Modesty, a Characteristic of Mary's Life	59
Eleventh Day—Mary at Bethlehem	66
Twelfth Day—Jesus Presented in the Temple by Mary	72
Thirteenth Day—The Life of the Holy Family	78
Fourteenth Day—Mary's Compassion	83
Fifteenth Day—Mary After the Resurrection	88
Sixteenth Day—Mary, Our Mother in the Cenacle	94

CONTENTS

	PAGE
Seventeenth Day—Mary, Our Mistress in the Cenacle	98
Eighteenth Day—Our Lady of the Cenacle	104
Nineteenth Day—Life of Adoration in Union with Mary	108
Twentieth Day—Mary's Adoration of Faith and Respect	114
Twenty-first Day—Mary's Adoration of Thanksgiving	118
Twenty-second Day—Mary's Eucharistic Contemplation	123
Twenty-third Day—Mary's Adoration of Propitiation	127
Twenty-fourth Day—Mary's Prayer of Adoration	132
Twenty-fifth Day—Mary's Apostolate	138
Twenty-sixth Day—The Divine Spouse and King of the Heart	144
Twenty-seventh Day—The Eucharist the Center of Mary's Life	149
Twenty-eighth Day—Mary's Life of Union with Jesus	154
Twenty-ninth Day—The Perfect Servant of the Blessed Sacrament	159
Thirtieth Day—Mary's Triumph	165
Last Day—Consecration to Our Lady of the Most Blessed Sacrament	172
Novena in Honor of Our Lady of the Most Blessed Sacrament	176
Litany of the Blessed Virgin	184

FOREWORD

The meditations in this book have been taken from the original sermon- or conference-notes of Blessed Eymard or from notes made by those who listened to his fervent instructions. He himself wrote very little *in extenso* and he did not write this month of Mary. It was compiled and arranged in its present form by one of his first companions, Rev. Albert Tesnière, S. S. S. It was thought advisable to leave the notes as much as possible in their original context, although this meant a certain amount of repetition. This very repetition, however, in a different context, has served to bring out Blessed Eymard's idea much more clearly.

Pope Pius X, of saintly memory, on December 30, 1905, wrote out with his own hand the prayer: *"Domina nostra Sanctissimi Sacramenti, ora pro nobis,"* and granted three hundred days' indulgence to the faithful for reciting this prayer: *"Our Lady of the Most Blessed Sacrament, pray for us."*

The Holy See has also granted permission to celebrate a feast in honor of our Lady of the Most Blessed Sacrament on May 13. As it has not approved as yet of a proper Mass and Office for this feast, the Mass and Office of the Common for feasts of the Blessed Virgin Mary are to be used.

An historical legend with appropriate practice and aspiration follows the meditation for each day of the month. Prayers for a novena in honor of our Lady of the Most Blessed Sacrament and the Litany of Loreto will be found in the last pages of this little book. As the late Cardinal Gibbons of Baltimore said in his approbation of the first American edition of this book, "The Reverend Clergy will find in the work appropriate readings for May devotions . . . that cannot fail to awaken sentiments of faith in the Real Presence, and of reverence for her who was raised to the sublime dignity of Mother of God."

In conformity with the decree of Urban VIII, March 13, 1625, we declare that we do not claim greater credibility for any of the extraordinary incidents herein related than is given to purely human testimony, except in those cases where Holy Church has decided otherwise. Furthermore we submit all that is said herein to the judgment of Holy Church whose obedient sons we wish ever to remain.

THE FATHERS OF THE
BLESSED SACRAMENT.

New York, March 25, 1930.

Our Lady of the Most Blessed Sacrament

PREPARATORY MEDITATION

The Month of Our Lady of the Most Blessed Sacrament

The Month of Mary is the month of blessings and of grace, for, as St Bernard, in company with all the Saints, assures us, all grace comes to us through Mary. The month of Mary is a continuous festival in honor of the Mother of God, which prepares us well for the beautiful month of the Blessed Sacrament which follows it.

I. Because our vocation calls us to give special honor to the Holy Eucharist, we must not for that reason give any the less devotion to the Blessed Virgin. Far from it! He would be guilty of blasphemy who would say, "The Most Blessed Sacrament suffices for me; I have no need of Mary." Where, then, shall we find Jesus on earth if not in Mary's arms? Was it not she who gave us the Eucharist! It was her consent to the Incarnation of the Word in her womb that inaugurated the great mystery of reparation to God and union with us which Jesus accomplished during His mortal life, and that He continues in the Eucharist.

Without Mary, we shall never find Jesus, for she possesses Him in her heart. There He takes His delight, and those who wish to know His inmost virtues, to experience the privilege of His intimate love, must seek these in Mary. They who love that good Mother find Jesus in her pure heart.

We must never separate Jesus from Mary; we can go to Him only through her.

I maintain, moreover, that the more we love the Eucharist, the more we must love Mary. We love all that our friend loves; now, was ever a creature better loved by God, a mother more tenderly cherished by her Son, than was Mary by Jesus?

O yes, our Lord would be much pained if we, the servants of the Eucharist, did not greatly honor Mary, because she is His Mother! Our Lord owes everything to her in the order of His Incarnation, His human nature. It is by the flesh that she gave Him that He has so glorified His Father, that He has saved us, and that He continues to nourish and save the world by the Blessed Sacrament.

Our Lord wishes us to honor her so much the more now, for that during His mortal life He seemed to neglect to do so Himself.

Our Lord certainly gave all honor to His Mother in His private life; but in public, He left her in the background, since He had ever and before all else to assert and maintain His dignity as God. But now our Lord wishes us, in a manner, to make up to the Most Blessed Virgin all that He did not do for her exteriorly: and we are bound (our eternal salvation is at stake) to honor her as the Mother of God and our Mother.

II. But since as adorers we are most especially consecrated to the service of the Eucharist, it is by virtue of this vocation that we owe a particular devotion to Mary. Religious of the Most Blessed Sacrament, Servants of the Blessed Sacrament, Associates of the Blessed Sacrament, we are, by reason of our profession, adorers of the Eucharist. This is our beautiful title, blessed by Pius IX. Adorers—what does this mean? It means that we are attached to the Adorable Person of our Lord living in the Eucharist. But if we belong to the Son, we belong to the Mother; if we adore the Son, we ought to honor the Mother: therefore we are obliged, in order to continue in the grace of our vocation and participate fully in it, to give very special honor to the Blessed Virgin under the title of OUR LADY OF THE MOST BLESSED SACRAMENT.

This devotion is not, as yet, much known, nor explicitly defined in the Church. But since devotion to Mary follows the worship of Jesus, it will also follow its various phases and developments.

When we honor our Lord on the Cross, we pray to our Lady of Seven Dolors. When we honor our Lord's humble, retired life of obedience at Nazareth, we may take for our Model, our Lady of the Hidden Life. The Blessed Virgin shares all the experiences of her Son.

We have not as yet invoked our Lady under this beautiful title, our Lady of the Most Blessed Sacrament; but devotion to the Eucharist is now spreading; it was never more vigorous or more widespread than in this our day. The devotion is growing everywhere, by day and by night; the Holy Eucharist will become a means of salvation for this age. The worship of the Eucharist is the glory, the power of this century.

And devotion to our Lady of the Most Blessed Sacrament will grow with the worship of the Eucharist.

I have not found this devotion treated of in any work; nor have I ever heard it spoken of, except in the Revelations of Mother Mary of Jesus, where I read something about Mary's Communions; and, again, in the Acts of the Apostles, where we find our Lady in the Cenacle.

III. What did the Blessed Virgin do in the Cenacle? She adored. She was the

Mother and the Queen of adorers. She was, in a word, our Lady of the Most Blessed Sacrament. Our occupation during this month will be to honor her under this beautiful title, to meditate on what she did, and to see how our Lord received her adoration. We shall discover the perfect union of these two hearts—that of Jesus with that of Mary—so merged as to seem one heart, one life. It is by our piety that we shall be enabled to penetrate that mysterious veil which surrounds the life of adoration of our Blessed Mother.

It is surprising that the Acts of the Apostles say nothing about this, but are satisfied with barely stating the fact that Mary dwelt in the Cenacle. Ah! it is, because her whole life there was one continuous act of love and adoration.

But how describe this love and adoration? how express that reign of God in the soul and that life of the soul in God? It cannot be portrayed. Language has no words wherewith to express the delights of heaven, and the same is true concerning the life of Mary in the Cenacle. Saint Luke tells us simply that she lived and prayed there.

Let us study her interior life at prayer, at adoration. We may picture to ourselves all that is most intense in love, all that is holiest and best in virtue, and then attribute all to Mary. And because Mary lived in the

Cenacle in union with the Most Blessed Sacrament for some twenty years, all her virtues bore the Eucharistic stamp. They were nourished by her Communions, by her adoration, and by her continual union with Jesus Eucharistic. Mary's virtues during her sojourn in the Cenacle reached their highest perfection—a perfection almost limitless—and were surpassed only by those of her Divine Son.

Let us ask our Lord to reveal to us what passed between Him and His Blessed Mother during those years in the Cenacle. He will make known to us some of those wonders— not all, for we could not bear to know all, but a few—and this knowledge will fill us with joy and admiration.

Oh! how happy I should be if I could but write some meditations on *A Month of Mary Adoratrix!* Much study would be necessary for that, much prayer, also. One must understand, furthermore, the thanksgiving of Mary's love. I greatly desire this, but for such a work a longer preparation would be required.

IV. All the mysteries of Mary's life are re-enacted in the Cenacle. If we meditate on the birth of her Son in Bethlehem let us continue the Gospel narrative, and soon we behold the Eucharistic birth of that same Son on the altar. Or if we take The Flight into Egypt: do we not see that our Lord is even now in the midst of strangers and barbarians, in those cities and countries in which the churches are closed and no one goes to visit Him? And then—His hidden life at Nazareth: do we not find Him even more hidden here? In this way consider all the other mysteries in the light of the Eucharist, and reflect on the part that Mary took therein.

The essential thing is to try to practice some given virtue of the Blessed Virgin's. Begin at once with the lowest, the smallest of these. When you have made them your own, you will go on, little by little, till you come to her interior virtues, even to that of her love.

Then let us daily offer up some sacrifice. Let us foresee something that will cost. There are some sacrifices that we can plan in advance: to see such a person, to perform such an act. Offer this sacrifice; the Blessed Virgin will be much pleased with it. It will be an added flower to the crown she wishes to offer to her Son, in our name, on His feast day—the beautiful feast of Corpus Christi.

If we foresee no particular sacrifice, let us maintain ourselves in the generous disposition to accept all that God will send us. Let us be vigilant in order that no occasion of denying ourselves may pass by us unnoticed. These are messengers from heaven, each bearing a grace and a crown of thorns.

We must welcome both. A sacrifice anticipated makes us reason, and reasoning diminishes its merit; but those that we accept generously without premeditation or deliberation are of more value. God wants to surprise us. He says to us: "Hold thyself in readiness!" and the faithful soul is ready to accept all that God wills. Love delights in surprises. Let us never lose these opportunities for sacrifice; all that is necessary is to be generous. A generous soul! What a beautiful thing in God's sight! God is glorified by such a one, and He says of her as He said of Job—with joy and admiration—"Hast thou seen My servant Job?" The soul that loves allows none of these daily sacrifices to pass. She is ever on the alert, her eyes heavenward. She feels that a cross is coming and she prepares to receive it.

Let us, then, honor the Blessed Virgin by a daily sacrifice. Let us go to our Lord through her; shelter ourselves behind her, take refuge beneath her protecting mantle; clothe ourselves in her virtues. Let us be, in short, but Mary's shadow. Let us offer all her actions, all her merits, all her virtues to our Lord. We have only to have recourse to Mary and to say to Jesus: "I offer Thee the riches that my good Mother has acquired for me"—and our Lord will be very much pleased with us.

THE CHAPLAIN OF OUR LADY OF THE MOST BLESSED SACRAMENT

We need a model, a patron, a guide in our devotion to our Lady of the Most Blessed Sacrament. We choose Saint John the Evangelist. Jesus had entrusted His Mother to him, and St John celebrated Holy Mass daily in the presence of Mary. Taking from the altar the Divine Bread, it was he who laid it upon Mary's lips: "Mother, behold thy son!" *Ecce filius tuus!* O God! what a word and what a moment! St John was the witness of Mary's adoration; he was the confidant of her love; and if he spoke so divinely of the Eucharist; if he sang the beautiful canticle of thanksgiving contained in the Gospel, it was because, after having received it from the mouth of Jesus, he had heard it repeated by Mary. "The Savior gave St John to Mary," says M. Olier, "not only that he might be a son to her in His place, but that he might by the Holy Mysteries he celebrated for her, and according to her intentions, give her the means of satisfying her heart's ardent desires for the establishment of the Church, and also to console her for her Son's absence by the happiness she felt in being nourished with Him every day." *(Vie de M. Olier, t. II, part. III, p. 207.)*

O glorious chaplain of the Cenacle, you will teach us to know the mysteries of the life of our Lady of the Most Blessed Sacrament; you will make us enter into her dispositions every time we receive or adore the God of the Eucharist.

Practice—Let us fulfill all our Eucharistic duties in union with our Lady of the Most Blessed Sacrament.

Aspiration—Hail, Mary, of whom was born Jesus Eucharistic!

FIRST DAY

Mary, Mother of Eucharistic Adorers

I. If our life were not under Mary's protection, we might have doubts as to our perseverance and our salvation. Our vocation, which, in a special manner, binds us to the service of the King of kings, makes it a more pressing duty for us to have recourse to Mary. Jesus is King in the Eucharist and He wishes only trained servitors in His court, only those who have served their apprenticeship. One must learn to serve before presenting oneself to the King! Therefore Jesus left us His Mother to be the Mother and Model of adorers. According to general opinion, He left her some twenty years on earth, that we might learn from her to adore Him perfectly. What a beautiful life—those twenty years spent in adoration! When we reflect upon our Lord's love for His Blessed Mother, we are lost in wonder that He consented to separate from her. Was it that the Blessed Virgin was not yet perfect? Was it that she had not suffered enough, she who had endured on Calvary more than all other creatures combined? Ah, yes, she had indeed suffered! But the interests of the Eucharist called for her presence. Jesus was not willing to remain alone in the Blessed Sacrament, without His Mother's Presence. He was not willing that the first hours of Eucharistic adoration should be confided to poor adorers, who knew not how to adore worthily. The Apostles, obliged to labor for the salvation of souls, could not give sufficient time to Eucharistic adoration. In spite of their love, which would have chained them to the Tabernacle, their Apostolic duties called them elsewhere. As for the newly made Christians, like unto children still in the cradle, a mother was needed to educate them, a model whom they could copy, and it was His Own Blessed Mother that Jesus left them as such.

II. All Mary's life—taken as a whole—may be summed up in this one word—adoration; for adoration is the perfect service of God, and it embraces all the duties of the creature toward the Creator.

It was Mary who first adored the Incarnate Word. He was in her womb, and no one on earth knew of it. Oh! how well was our Lord served in Mary's virginal womb! Never has He found a ciborium, a golden vase more precious or purer than was Mary's womb! Mary's adoration was more pleasing to Him than that of all the Angels. The Lord "hath set His tabernacle in the sun," says the Psalmist. That sun is Mary's heart.

At Bethlehem, Mary was the first to adore her Divine Son lying in the manger. She adored Him with the perfect love of a Virgin Mother, the love of charity, as says the Holy Spirit. After Mary, St Joseph, the shepherds, then the Magi came to adore: but it was Mary who opened up that furrow of fire that was to spread over the world. And what beautiful things, what divine things, Mary must have said! for hers was an ardent love whose depths we can never fathom.

Mary continued to adore our Lord: first in His hidden life at Nazareth; afterwards in His apostolic life; and, finally, on Calvary, where her adoration became intense suffering. Notice the nature of Mary's adoration. She adored our Lord according to the different states of His life; Jesus' state determined the character of her adoration—her adoration did not stay in a set groove. At one time, she adored God annihilated in her womb; at another, as poor and lowly in Bethlehem; again, as laboring at Nazareth; and later on, as evangelizing the country and converting sinners. She adored Him in His sufferings on Calvary by suffering with Him. Her adoration was always in keeping with the sentiments of her Divine Son, which were clearly revealed to her. Her love brought her into perfect conformity of thought and life with Him.

III. To you, adorers, we say: Always

adore Jesus Eucharistic, but vary your adoration as the Blessed Virgin did hers. Recall to your mind all the mysteries of religion in connection with the Eucharist, so as to avoid routine. If your love is not nourished by a new form of devotion, a new thought, you will become stupid in prayer. We should for this reason commemorate *all* the mysteries in the Eucharist.

It was thus Mary prayed in the Cenacle.

When the anniversaries of the great mysteries, wrought under her very eye, came round, it is impossible for us to think that she did not recall their circumstances—the words, the graces. When, for instance, Christmas came, can we imagine Mary's not reminding her Son, now hidden under the Eucharistic Veil, of the love that greeted Him at His birth, of her smiles, of her adoration and that of St Joseph, the shepherds, the Magi? She wished, thereby, to rejoice the Heart of Jesus by reminding Him of her love. And so with all the other mysteries.

How, then, do we act with a friend? Do we always speak to him of the present? Certainly not! We recall past memories, we live them over again together. When we want to pay a compliment to a father and a mother we recall their love, their unwearying devotedness shown us in our infancy. Similarly, Mary, during her adoration in the Cenacle, reminded Jesus of all that He had done for His Father's glory, all the great sacrifices He had made, and in this way she participated in the Eucharistic grace.

The Eucharist is the memorial of all the mysteries of religion; it renews their love and their grace. And so we must, like Mary, correspond to this grace by contemplating our Lord in all His actions, by adoring and uniting ourselves with Him in all the different states of His life.

The Eucharist had so powerful an attraction for the Blessed Virgin that she could not live away from It. She lived in It and by It. She passed her days and her nights at the feet of her Divine Son. She did, indeed, gratify the filial devotion of the Apostles and the Faithful who desired to see and converse with her, but her love for her hidden God shone in her countenance and communicated its ardor to all about her.

O Mary! teach us the life of adoration! Teach us to see, as thou didst, all the mysteries and all the graces in the Eucharist; to live over again the Gospel story and to read it in the light of the Eucharistic Life of Jesus. Remember, O our Lady of the Most Blessed Sacrament, that thou art the Mother of all adorers of the Holy Eucharist.

OUR MODELS

Among the holy personages who shed luster on the eighteenth century, we find several who teach us how we may join worship of the Eucharist to devotion to Mary and uphold one by the other.

The venerable Cardinal de Bérulle, on whom the title of "Apostle of the Incarnate Word" was bestowed by Pope Urban VIII, and whose views on the Most Blessed Virgin appear to be more angelic than human; and also Father de Condren, who, according to the most able Doctors of his time, received sublime lights on these mysteries, had the habit of offering Holy Mass every Saturday in honor of the Blessed Virgin. M. Olier, the holy founder of St Sulpice, and reformer of the clergy at the same time, got from them this pious custom. He had three Masses celebrated every day, the intention of each Mass being placed in the Blessed Virgin's hands, that she might, in offering it to her Son for the Church, obtain infinite treasures of grace.

There was also a pious Jesuit missionary in Quebec who proposed to Blessed John Eudes, founder of the Congregation bearing his name, a plan for an association of priests, whom he called our Lady's Chaplains, and who were to unite in offering the Holy Sacrifice for the intentions of the august Queen of Heaven, so that, as he put it, the Son of God would ascend to His Father, in the Host, through the very pure hands of the one whom He had used to come down to us in becoming man. (*Vie de M. Olier, t.* II *passim.*)

Practice—Offer our adoration to Jesus Eucharistic through the hands of Mary.

Aspiration—Thou art blessed amongst women, O Mary, and Blessed is Jesus Eucharistic, the fruit of thy womb!

SECOND DAY

The Immaculate Conception and Holy Communion

Mary's Immaculate Conception was foretold in the terrestrial Paradise. The Most Holy Virgin is that blessed woman who was to crush with her heel the head of the infernal serpent. God in creating Mary immaculate, scores His great victory over the devil; He reëstablishes His sovereignty over the earth. God reënters creation as Master!

It was primarily for His own glory that God preserved Mary from the taint of original sin, for in all His works God seeks first of all the interests of His glory. Every creature being born into the world with the guilt and stain of sin, God was not completely Master, He could not entirely dominate it. Satan seized upon the soul at the very moment of its creation. God created, and Satan took possession of His work. God's glory was humiliated in His creatures. And when the Lord drove Adam and Eve out of the Garden of Paradise, Satan had triumphed over God: it was his victory.

But behold Mary! God protects her, preserves her by a most special privilege. She

SECOND DAY

was conceived in a natural manner, like all mankind since Adam, but God owed it to Himself to keep her unsullied. Eve, the first mother, was defiled; Mary, the true Mother of the living, will be immaculate. God overshadows her; she is His garden enclosed, His fountain sealed up, of whose waters the King alone shall drink. Satan dare not approach Mary, born in the arms of God's love: *Dominus possedit me in initio viarum suarum*—true daughter of God! *Primogenita ante omnem creaturam.* The Word must not blush for His mother.

God gave her *everything:* in looking at Mary, God beheld His honor and His glory. The Most Holy Trinity concurred in the Immaculate Conception of Mary; the glory of the Three Divine Persons demanded it: could Satan have anticipated God, Satan would have been victor, for no matter how great the rehabilitation, the person born to slavery always bears the marks.

But in this way the glory of God was reëstablished in humanity; God's image was remodeled and restored. God may now, without fear, come down and take up His abode in Mary, for she is a tabernacle purer than the sun. Mary is, by her purity, God's paradise: with her He will renew the world.

See what the Immaculate Conception has given us: first of all—Jesus Christ; Mary is the aurora of the beautiful Sun of Justice.

Then, the Saints, those brilliant stars in the firmament of the Church. All have been formed through Mary; everything comes to us through this paradise of the Lord. The Immaculate Conception is the source of all the grace that we have received. Of herself, Mary is but a speck on the horizon, like the little cloud seen by Elias; but she grows, she expands, until her divine influence pervades the whole world.

II. But for us, adorers, there is something more in this mystery of the Immaculate Conception. If God thus preserved Mary, it was because He wished to dwell in her; He willed to come to earth and take up His abode in a holy dwelling-place, pure and undefiled. The Eternal Father and the Holy Spirit sanctified Mary in order to make her a worthy tabernacle for the Divine Word: for this it was necessary to create another heaven; Mary *had* to be immaculate in order to receive the Word into her being. The Immaculate Conception is the remote preparation for Holy Communion. Oh! with what complacence did not the Word contemplate that dwelling which He had prepared for Himself! He hastens to it with rapid steps: *Exultavit ut gigas.*

Jesus should experience the same joy when He comes to us in Holy Communion. He should long for the moment when we cause Him to be taken from the Tabernacle;

He should be able to come to us with the same delight as though it were again to Mary that He came. He will, if we are pure. He expects nothing else of us but this preparation of purity. Great purity, then, in the reception of Holy Communion, should be for us the fruit of the Immaculate Conception. Without it, all other virtues are of no avail; if that be wanting, our Lord will come to us with repugnance, our soul will be but a prison to Him. "Ah!" He will say to His priest, "whither are you carrying Me? Into a heart that is not Mine, that my enemy occupies? Leave Me, leave Me in My Tabernacle!"

O Mary, lend us thy mantle of purity; clothe us in the whiteness, in the glory of thy Immaculate Conception! It behooves the mother to adorn her child for festive occasion. Clothed by thee, O Mary, Jesus will welcome me; He will come to me with pleasure, for He will see thee in me, and He will find His delight in dwelling in my heart.

THE BLESSED VIRGIN ASKS THAT THE MOST HOLY EUCHARIST BE HONORED

Florence—1230

In a Benedictine Monastery in Florence, in December 1230, a drop of consecrated wine, left in the chalice by a venerable priest, whose eyesight had become weakened by age, was at the moment of the ablutions suddenly changed into crimson blood.

Three days later another miracle took place: this drop of wine, which had changed into blood and had been put into a crystal vial with the ablution, took on the appearance of human flesh and remained suspended by its own power, without in any way touching the crystal sides of the container; at the same time the unconsecrated wine which had served for the ablutions and which filled about half of the vial, took on the tint of rose-colored water and instantly dried up without leaving a trace of dampness.

A voice from Heaven twice claimed honors for this miraculous Particle. The first time was to the Bishop of Florence himself. While asleep, an extraordinary voice addressed him three different times: "O Bishop, thou didst receive Me naked and thou didst send Me away naked"; thus reproaching him for his hardness of heart and his irreverence toward the holy relic momentarily in his possession, and which he had returned without honors to the monastery that claimed It. To repair his fault he ordered a magnificent Tabernacle of ivory, inlaid with gold and covered with purple, to be used as a dwelling-place for the Body of the Savior.

Another warning from Heaven soon came, to require new honors for the miraculous Sacrament. The most holy Virgin, who still watches over the Eucharistic crib, as she watched over the restingplace of her Divine Child in Bethlehem, appeared in a dream to a young child in the monastery where the miracle took place, and said to her: "Go and find Sister Marguerite (she was the sacristan and later became Abbess of Ripoli) and let her know that the sacred Object of the Almighty Power of my Son Jesus lies without shelter very near this church." Ildebandesca obeyed the Blessed Virgin and fulfilled her mission that morning: enlightened from above, Sister Marguerite had understood at once the mysterious message. A rich ciborium was immediately ordered from some skillful artificers, and the Bishop came himself and placed within it the miraculous and Most Holy Sacrament with all due honors. *(Les Miracles historiques du Saint Sacrement, par le P. Eugène Couet.)*

Practice—I will prepare myself most carefully for Holy Communion in union with my Mother, Mary.

Aspiration—Jesus Hostia loves the sacred dwelling of Mary's womb more than all the tabernacles of Jacob.

THIRD DAY

The Dowry of Mary Immaculate

I. On the day of her Immaculate Conception, Mary received a magnificent dowry in keeping with her sublime duties and her incomparable dignity as Mother of God. She received then that treasure of grace which was to make her the co-redemptrix of mankind, partner in the work of our salvation.

Without doubt the grace of the Immaculate Conception surpasses all the other graces conferred on Mary, even that of her divine maternity. Though less in dignity, it is more important before God and more important for Mary; it is, moreover, the foundation and the source of all the privileges afterwards accorded her. It would have been of little account to be the Mother of God, and, at the same time, a sinner. What constitutes greatness in God's sight, is not the dignity that He confers, but the sanctity and purity with which it is borne. Throw a royal mantle around a beggar and he still remains a beggar. The Immaculate Conception having assured Mary's purity and sanctity, it is the greatest of her graces.

From the first instant of her creation, Mary was more pleasing to God than all other creatures. One act of love from that frail creature still hidden in the maternal womb, gave more glory to God than the united love of all the Angels and Saints. The profits are always in proportion to the capital; and Mary possessed a fund of immeasurable graces that yielded a hundredfold.

II. The Immaculate Conception is the starting point of all Mary's virtues. It is her dominating virtue in the sense that she ever labored to fructify the abundance of its grace.

We may state it as a principle that she was never unfaithful to the slightest inspiration of the Holy Spirit, and that she cooperated to the fullest extent with all the graces that were given her. No saint was ever so faithful. We always fall short of what grace expects of us. For this reason the Angel declared Mary *"Full of grace." "The Lord is with thee,"* he tells her—with thee always and in all things. There is no void that grace has not filled. Ah! Mary was faithful to all her obligations, faithful to all the desires of the Lord! She never missed an opportunity of practicing virtue. She welcomed all the rays of God's holiness, absorbing them into her being without letting anything be lost.

This fidelity to grace made Mary advance

without ceasing in virtue. Mary kept watch over her fund of graces as though there had been fear of losing them. What a lesson for us! Whatever our graces may be, let us guard them well! Mary, who was impeccable, not by nature, but because of her union with God; Mary, whom temptation never approached, kept a strict guard over herself and labored incessantly at the work of her sanctification. Hers was one continuous progress in virtue. She retired to the Temple at the age of three in order to shun the scandals of the world. She trembled before an Angel, a pure spirit, who spoke only of God. Mary never thought that she had done enough. Her later life was one prolonged martyrdom without the least alleviation. Mary embroidered the robe of her Immaculate Conception; she enriched and ornamented it with the beautiful flowers of her virtues; it was always this initial grace that she developed and embellished by her sacrifices.

III. The Immaculate Conception is, again, the measure of her power and glory. It is only through our purity and holiness that we can prevail with God. God can only accomplish great things in pure souls; He hears only the innocent or the pardoned. Mary's purity had never been tarnished by the slightest spot; what, then, must not her influence be! They say that a mother's influence is all-powerful over the heart of her son. Alas! should she herself be dishonored, what becomes of her influence? But what can one refuse a mother who is pure! Solomon said to his mother after she had done penance: *"I can refuse you nothing."* What, then, can Mary's Son refuse her! All grace passes through her hands; she is the reservoir. Jesus has placed in her hands His Almighty power in the order of salvation.

And Mary's glory? Her purity won for her the privilege of becoming the Mother of the King, and to-day, she is enthroned at the right of her Son in heaven. She receives all possible honor and homage, short of adoration. She is so beautiful, so glorious that she might well herself make the bliss of paradise!

IV. Thus all Mary's grace and virtue, all her power and glory, proceed from her Immaculate Conception. They are, so to speak, its magnificent dowry. Baptism purifies us, makes us stainless. As soon as the child receives this Sacrament, he becomes the temple of God, a paradise. With what watchful care should we not guard our Baptismal innocence! If we have lost it, then we must purify ourselves by penance. We *must* be pure. I do not speak merely of the purity of the senses; we must observe great purity in all our actions; have great purity of will, of intention; possess purity of life throughout—everything lies in that. Without purity, we can never please the Eucharistic God, for He is purity itself. Only the pure of heart can see Him, can pierce the veil that hides Him. He shows Himself to the pure of heart alone, for purity is love, that delicacy of affection that would never wish to give the least offense. Our Lord's work in coming into our souls is to purify us more and more: in purifying us, He makes us holy; in making us holy, He unites us more closely with Himself. When we are pure enough, He will take us to Himself in heaven and there crown us with immortal glory.

MARY WATCHES OVER THE SACRED HOSTS

Paterno (Italy)—1772

On January 28, 1772, the village of Saint Pierre de Paterno, situated about two miles from Naples, was the scene of a frightful sacrilege. Thieves carried away from the Tabernacle two ciboriums containing a hundred consecrated Hosts. It was only through a miraculous intervention that these Hosts were found. Lights appeared over both places where they had been buried. First, on the morning of the 26th of the following February, a priest from Naples digging into the earth at the foot of a poplar tree, whence a dazzling light had burst forth, had the consolation of recovering forty of them. Notwithstanding a most severe winter and heavy rains they were white, intact, and in a perfect state of preservation, the edges only having been slightly stained with mud. Moreover, the earth which had come in contact with the Body of Jesus Christ, and which had been gathered absolutely dry into a clean linen cloth, began to give forth clear water. On the evening of the following Thursday the rest of the stolen Hosts were found in the same miraculous manner; they were as perfectly preserved as the ones previously discovered.

It is fitting to cite here the following testimony which we owe to the parish priest of Paterno, Matthias d'Anna, and which is the echo of an unchanging tradition in that part of the country. During the interval which elapsed between the sacrilegious theft and the apparition of the lights, a mule-driver named Francis Jodice, twenty-seven years old, whose custom it was to return to Naples towards evening, often saw in the field where the sacred Hosts had been buried, a lady leaning against a tree. One evening he plucked up courage and asked her what she was doing all alone in that field. "I am here," she replied, "to watch over my Son." When the consecrated Hosts were found, everyone understood clearly that the lady was the Most Blessed Virgin Mary.

As to the sacred Hosts around which the Divine Power had multiplied these wonders, the Vicar General of Naples made the canonical examination, and placed them in two crystal cylinders closed with silver bands, so that later they might be exposed for the veneration of the Faithful. *(Les Miracles historiques du Saint Sacrement, par le P. Eugène Couet.)*

Practice—In all our Communions we should ask for the purity of a perfect life through the intercession of Mary Immaculate.

Aspiration—We sing thy praises, O Mary, thou glorious city of the Eucharistic God!

FOURTH DAY

The Nativity of the Blessed Virgin

Let us rejoice at the birth of our Queen and Mother, which filled heaven with joy, earth with hope, and hell with terror! Behold, at last *"the strong woman,"* the predestined Mother of the Messiah!

No mention is made of the place or circumstances connected with her birth, but we may readily suppose that, like her Divine Son, she was born in poverty. St Joachim and St Ann were poor. They belonged to the Levitical family, and lived on the tithes of the Temple. However, Mary was born with a splendor far surpassing all the riches of the daughters of this world.

I. Mary possessed worldly greatness. She was born the daughter, the sister, and the heiress of the kings of Juda. The Word willed to be born of a royal mother. He willed to be, according to the flesh, the brother of kings, in order to show to the world that from Him all royalty comes, and that kings should acknowledge Him as their Master and Sovereign Ruler. His Mother was, therefore, a Queen. As her Son was a King without an earthly kingdom, without riches or armies, so was she poor and unknown. Earthly pomp does not constitute royalty, that is only its outward show; but even when sovereignty is not acknowledged, its rights still exist. However, the day was to come on which Mary's royalty, as that of her Son, would be proclaimed and receive due honor. The Church was to salute her as Queen—Queen of heaven and earth: *"Salve, Regina!"* The Angel had announced it: *"Dabit illi Dominus Deus sedem David patris ejus"*—"The Lord, O Mary, will give to thy Son the throne of David, His Father." But before that day should come, He had to win it back by a life of humility, poverty and suffering.

II. Mary possessed all supernatural greatness. Supernatural greatness is but the reflection of God upon a creature whom He associates with Himself in power and glory. Now, what did God do for Mary? He associates her with His great mystery. The Father calls her His daughter, the Son loves her as His Mother, while the Holy Ghost guards her as His spouse. She was destined to share in the great work of divine power. She is associated with the empire of God Himself. Let us contemplate her, then, as such, on the beautiful day of her birth. With St John, let us see her, clothed with the sun, *amicta sole,* coming from the Hand of God, resplendent with His divine light. She is, as it were, penetrated with the rays of the Divinity, like unto a pure crystal into which the sunbeam enters. The moon is under her feet, typifying her unshakable power which defies inconstancy, for she has vanquished, once and forever, the infernal dragon. Her brow is encircled with a diadem of twelve stars,—the graces and virtues of the elect, for Mary is the center of creation. Jesus has confided to her all the means of salvation, and she is honored by all the Saints, who are the work of her love and her protection.

III. Mary was born with all personal greatness. She was enriched with God's choicest gifts. But on the day of her birth, she was already rich in her own right; she had already acquired treasures of merit during the nine months of silent, uninterrupted adoration in her mother's womb. Even before birth, she was penetrated with divine light, she had given herself to God completely. She loved Him with a love of which we can form no adequate idea; and she was born with the treasures that she had acquired, with the riches she had coined. Oh! if we could have seen in spirit the birth of Mary, have seen this sun coming up out of the ocean of God's love! In her mind, the most pure light; in her heart, the most ardent love; in her will, the most absolute devotion. Never had any other creature such a birth!

Even in her cradle, Mary was the delight of the Most Holy Trinity, the admiration of the Angels. "Who is this privileged one," they ask, "who at the first dawn of life, is so rich in virtue and adorned with such glory?"—*Quæ est ista?*

And the demons tremble; they behold her advancing against them, "strong as an army in battle array": they feel the humiliation of their leader's defeat and they already foresee the terrible war that this child of a day will wage against them: *Sicut acies ordinata.*

But the world rejoices, for it beholds the advent of its liberatrix. Mary's birth heralds that of the Savior. O yes, truly let us rejoice! *Nativitas tua gaudium annuntiavit universo mundo.*

In like manner should we rejoice, since Mary brings us the Bread of Life. From the day of her birth we salute her as the aurora of the Eucharist, for we know that the Savior of mankind will take from her the substance of that Body and Blood which He will give us in the Adorable Sacrament of His love.

ST PETER OF VERONA AND THE MANICHEES

A wealthy Catholic of Milan was accustomed to offer hospitality to St Peter of Verona, when on his apostolic journeys. One evening St Peter arrived completely worn out with fatigue. His host, usually so hospitable and reverential, almost shut the door on him. What could be the meaning of the change? Finally, in the course of conversation his host confides his trouble. A Manichean heretic had come to see him, had reproached him for the hospitality that he had given to "the enemy of the truth," and had finally said: "Come with me; I will show you the Blessed Virgin, who will tell you more about this." His curiosity getting the better of him, he accompanied the man to the sectarian meeting. A dazzling lady appeared on the altar, holding her son in her arms. "My son," she said, "you are in error; you can see the truth is with us, and not with the Catholics. I, the Mother of Jesus, tell you this." Convinced, the unfortunate man became a Manichean.

"Go and tell the man who spoke to you, that I also will become a Manichean if he will show me the Blessed Virgin," said St Peter. His host hastened to inform his new friend, who accepted with joy. St Peter passed the night in prayer. The next morning at Mass he reserved one of the consecrated Hosts, which he enclosed in a pyx and then placed reverently on his breast. Thus armed, he set out for the Manichean meeting. The person who took the part of medium caused the dazzling lady to appear on the altar. She reproached the new arrival with his ignorance of the truth. Whereupon St Peter, raising aloft the Holy Host, said to the apparition: "If you are truly the Mother of God, adore thy Son!" At these words, the phantom disappeared in a cloud of black smoke, leaving the hall filled with a foul smell. The demon had fled before his Master. *(Les Miracles historiques du Saint Sacrement.)*

Practice—Let us offer to God, by the hands of Mary, the fruits of the Holy Sacrifice of the Mass.

Aspiration—Hail, Mary, who brought us from afar our Bread of Life, the Divine Victim!

FIFTH DAY

Mary's Presentation in the Temple

I. Mary had no childhood in the ordinary sense of the word. She had no games, no childish taste, none of the inconstancy or inexperience of childhood. From her very conception she possessed perfect knowledge of God and she acquired merit. All her faculties were directed towards God, for He was her very life. Her body alone had the frailty and stature of childhood. As soon as she could walk alone, she asked her parents' permission to retire to the Temple. She was but three years old when she was received there among the pious maidens who were consecrated to the Lord, and there she remained for twelve years. We know nothing of her life in the Temple except that she lived a secluded life and that she practiced every virtue. Certain saintly Doctors of the Church, St John Damascene among others, assert that she preferred the company of those children who suffered, taking care of them in their illnesses, consoling them in their little troubles. If any quarrel arose, little Mary was always called to conciliate the disputants and impart to them that peace which she carried with her wherever she went. She lived a very simple life, not drawing attention to herself in any way. She was the servant of all, never losing courage, and anticipating the desires of her young companions. She was protected by angels and surrounded by heavenly spirits. The demon dared not approach her, shielded as she was by her faithful guardians. She was that *"enclosed garden"* which none but the well-beloved Spouse could enter.

II. It is in her hidden life in the Temple that Mary should be our model. God had prepared her in secret, in silence, without her even suspecting the great mission that she was to fulfill. Later on, our Lord in the same manner prepares Himself for His evangelical mission by thirty years of prayerful seclusion at Nazareth. For three years He prepares His Apostles and disciples for the mystery of the Eucharist, and it was on the eve of His death only that He revealed to them all Its love.

Silence and seclusion are the soul of great things. Our Lord hid from Satan the fact that He was the Son of God. Had the demon been positive of this, he would never have urged the Jews to put Him to death. Nor was he aware that this young maiden was one day to be the Mother of God. So long as a work remains hidden, unknown to the world, it grows in security; but as soon as the devil discovers it and makes it known to the world, he inveighs against it and combats it with all his might. If the seed cast into the soil is too often disturbed, it will not grow: it must be allowed to remain hidden under the earth. So it is with us; if we wish to grow we must hide ourselves, we must remain unknown to the world, otherwise the demon will raise up many contradictions and the breath of self-love will destroy us.

III. Our Lord has prepared us a long time. He has hedged us about with graces from our infancy, in order to introduce us into the Cenacle of His Eucharist. Let us thank Him with all our heart. Although we may not have given ourselves to Him at so early an age as Mary, we are, however, still in the beginning of the Eucharistic life. The Eucharistic manifestation has only just begun, and our Lord calls us to be among the first to work for its development.

Mary adored God in the Temple in spirit and in truth. By her prayers and ardent desires she hastened the coming of the Messiah. But we adore Him really present on our Altars; we do not call Him from afar, as Mary did. He is in our midst; He is with us always. Let us imitate the silence, the solitude, the hidden life of our Blessed Mother.

Nowadays we are content just to appear

the thing; we wish to attain and to enjoy *at once;* we don't know how to wait. We force the plant; it springs up quickly at first, but in a very little while it has exhausted itself, and so dies.

Let us, then, love the simple, hidden life, the obscure employments of our state in life; let us find our happiness in being unknown; let us hide the tiny flame of our lamp under a bushel, for the least breath of wind may extinguish it.

Mary gave herself to God promptly, unreservedly, and forever. She gave Him her mind, her heart, her liberty—she kept nothing back. Oh, let us give all to Jesus Eucharistic, who gives Himself entirely to us. It is easy enough to say, "My God, I give myself entirely to Thee," but it is difficult to do so in reality. Let us rely on His grace and on our Mother's intercession, and when opportunity offers, let us recall her perfect oblation of herself to God. Her example will be our strength and encouragement.

WE MUST NEVER SEPARATE MARY FROM JESUS

Saint Hyacinth of the Order of Friar Preachers, hearing that the Tartars were about to attack the City of Kiew, where he dwelt, ran to the convent church and secured the holy ciborium, to save his Divine Master from the ungodliness of these barbarous Infidels. As he was leaving the church carrying his treasure away, a very large and heavy statue of Mary, which stood near the door, called him three times. Hyacinth, astonished, asked the Blessed Virgin what she wanted of him; and Mary answered thus: "My beloved Hyacinth, do you wish to save the Son from barbarous outrages and to abandon the Mother to their insults?" On the Saint's pleading his weakness as the excuse for not carrying so heavy a statue, Mary answered: "Oh, if thou hadst a little love, it would be easy for thee to take me away; pray to my Son; He will make the burden light for thee." The Saint at once took the statue and carried it as easily as though it had been a little flower.

The Blessed Sacrament on his breast, the statue of Mary in his arms, he crossed the enemy's lines unmolested, and directing his steps towards Cracovia arrived there safely.

Practice—Let us repeat incessantly: "Mary and Jesus! Jesus and Mary!"

Aspiration—"They found the Child with Mary His Mother, and falling down they adored Him."

SIXTH DAY

The Annunciation

When we reflect on the circumstances connected with the mystery of the Annunciation, we realize the incomparable glory it was for Mary to have been chosen to co-operate in the work of the Incarnation of the Word—the grandest of all divine works! And what virtues her example teaches us!

I. An Archangel is deputed by God to treat with a humble creature. It is the most important mission ever fulfilled by one of these celestial spirits. The Angel, beautiful as a star, radiant with heavenly splendor, comes down to earth.

To whom does he go? Ah, had the world known of the heavenly visitant's coming to earth, it would have sought among the rich and the powerful for the happy mortal for whom he bore the wondrous message. The world believes only too willingly that perfection is found in greatness. But the Angel seeks out a lowly virgin of fifteen, humble and unknown, espoused to a poor artisan, dwelling in a despised, out-of-the-way village. He comes to Mary! What! so much ceremony for this unknown maiden! Yes—

worldly prestige does not amount to so much, after all, does it? This rather sets at defiance our human standards! We only see the things that dazzle; we only put a value on such things as gold and diamonds. But what do things such as these amount to? In the Eternal values they are only fit to trample under foot like worthless pebbles—hell is paved with just such things.

So the Angel comes to a virgin. God admits only pure souls to His friendship. He pardons the sinner, but He unites Himself only to purity.

The Angel is the first to salute. His is, indeed, the lesser dignity of the two. Mary is sovereign here, and since the Three Divine Persons are awaiting her answer, she holds the world's fate in her hands. Ah, how powerful is that lowly maiden!

"Hail, full of grace!" Among all the daughters of Eve, Mary alone is full of grace. We are full of the miseries resulting from original sin. But Mary is pure as the sun; God formed her of a special earth, and fashioned her with particular care.

"The Lord is with thee." Yes, for He dwells in the purity of thy heart, O Mary, as in a paradise of delight, and thy virtues are as so many flowers that send up to Him the sweetest fragrance. At what hour did the Angel appear? The Gospel does not say, but many commentators think that it was

at midnight, at that moment when one day ends and another begins, for Mary is the aurora that separates light from darkness. Mary was at that moment at prayer, pleading for the coming of the Messiah—at least, we may suppose so without fear of deceiving ourselves, for God generally gives to souls a power of prayer in keeping with the grace He wishes to confer on them, in order to prepare them for this. Let us, then, at this solemn hour of the Conception, as also later at the birth of the Son of God, pray with Mary, our Mother, and in union with her adore the God who became Incarnate for us.

II. Mary was troubled. It is the nature of virgins, says St Ambrose, to be troubled at the approach of man, and to fear his words. Mary was troubled at the words of praise addressed to her, although she well deserved them. But true virtue never recognizes itself.

The Angel reassures Mary. It is characteristic of divine visions first to trouble, then to give peace; whereas those from the evil one begin peacefully and end in warfare.

"Thou shalt conceive a Son and thou shalt call His Name Jesus." Heavenly Name! Divine Name, that no man could give; that had to be brought from heaven by an Angel! This Son will be powerful. He shall be called the Angel of the Great Council, the

Mighty One, the Admirable One. But the Blessed Virgin still hesitates. She treasures so the virginity she has vowed to God. "How," says she, "can this mystery be accomplished? I am, and I wish to remain a virgin." What a moment! Mary holds Heaven and earth in suspense; God awaits the consent of this humble maiden! God cannot proceed without her: Mary in this moment is more powerful than God Himself. How could God deign to accept this sort of inferiority before Mary? Ah! it is because He values Mary's virginity before everything.

The Angel then yields to Mary in God's Name. Mary has triumphed! She hears his words: "The power of the Most High shall overshadow thee; in becoming a mother, thou shalt remain a virgin."

III. And Mary replies: *"Ecce ancilla Domini"*—"Behold the handmaid of the Lord! Be it done to me according to thy word!" O word full of deep significance! O admirable word full of humility! How much is contained in that one word: *"Ecce!"* When the priest presents the Sacred Host to us before Holy Communion, he says: *"Ecce Agnus Dei!"* When St John the Baptist wished to point out our Lord to his disciples, he exclaimed: *"Ecce!"* In that word is contained the total oblation of one's self: Here am I, all ready; entirely at God's service! It is a perfect act of faith.

Mary did not say: Behold the Mother of the Lord! although at that moment she was actually His Mother. The higher God raises the Saints, the humbler they are in their own estimation. With reason, then, does St Bernard say of Mary: *"Virginitate placuit, humilitate concepit"*—"She pleased the Lord by her virginity, she conceived Him by her humility."

Let us take note of how sparing Mary was of her words. She said only what was strictly necessary, nothing more. Silence and modesty are the safeguards of purity.

The Holy Spirit accomplishes in Mary His divine work. The consent of this young maiden has changed the face of the world. God reënters His domain. He takes up His intercourse with man again, but in a way much more perfect and enduring than in the terrestrial Paradise.

This mystery of the Annunciation ennobles us, for it brings God back to earth. It is, at the same time, a mystery entirely interior, a mystery of Communion. In Communion, Jesus Eucharistic becomes, in a manner, Incarnate in us, and Communion is the object of His Incarnation. By communicating worthily we enter into the Divine plan, we complete it. The Incarnation prepared the way for and heralded Transubstantiation. Mary did not receive the Word for herself alone. She rejoiced that we should be able to participate in her happiness. Let us, then, unite ourselves with her when we receive Jesus. Let us sing her *Magnificat*. The Lord, in this mystery, has done great things in Mary; and He has also done great things in coming to us. Let us strive to imitate her virtues so that Jesus Christ may find in us, as in His holy Mother, a dwelling worthy of Him.

MARY REWARDS ST ANDREW CORSINI'S DEVOTION TO THE HOLY EUCHARIST

Saint Andrew Corsini, already illustrious for his virtue and holiness, was, after the repeated demands of the people, raised to the dignity of Holy Orders, notwithstanding the resistance due to his humility. When the day of his first Mass came, his parents wished him to celebrate it with all possible pomp in the city church. But the Saint obtained permission from his Superior to retire secretly into a solitary convent, hidden in the heart of a forest. It was there that he offered his first Sacrifice, lost in his love for the Sacred Host he immolated. The Saint's courageous course was so pleasing to Mary, that appearing to him immediately after the Communion, she said to him: "Andrew, you are my servant. I have chosen you, and I will glorify myself in you."

This good Mother manifested by this favor that nothing pleases her so much as the love and respect we testify for her Divine Son present in the Blessed Sacrament for love of us. *(Bolland. 5 February.)*

Practice—We should try to avoid any word, any noise, any distraction, when in the presence of the Blessed Sacrament.

Aspiration—The fruit of my womb, Jesus in the Sacred Host, is more precious than the purest gold or the costliest gems.

SEVENTH DAY

The First Adorer of the Incarnate Word

Behold my model, my Mother, Mary, the first adorer of the Incarnate Word in her womb! O how perfect must this adoration of the Virgin Mother have been; how pleasing to God, and how rich in grace!

In what did the perfection of Mary's adoration consist, at the first moment of the Incarnation?

It was an adoration of humility, of self-annihilation before the sovereign majesty of God because, impelled by so much benevolence and love for her and all mankind, He had made choice of her, His humble handmaid, to be the Mother of the Messiah. Of such nature should be our first act of adoration after having received Holy Communion; such were the sentiments of St Elizabeth when receiving the Mother of God, who bore the Savior in her womb: *"Unde hoc mihi?"* "Whence comes to me this happiness; which I so little deserve?" Of such sort, also, were the words of the Centurion, with whom Jesus would have made His sojourn: "Lord, I am not worthy!"

II. The second of Mary's acts of adoration would naturally be one of joyous gratitude for God's ineffable and infinite goodness to man; an act of humble gratitude for His having chosen her, His unworthy handmaid, for so signal a favor. Her gratitude was voiced in fervent acts of loving praise and thanksgiving. Gratitude is an outpouring of the soul, the loving expansion of a noble soul—it is the heart of love.

III. The third act of the Blessed Virgin's adoration would have been an act of oblation, of self-sacrifice: the entire gift of herself, of her life, to the service of God: *Ecce ancilla Domini;* an act of regret to be so little able to serve Him in a worthy manner. She offered herself to God to serve Him in whatever manner He willed: by all the sacrifices that He might be pleased to ask of her, too happy to be able to please Him at any price and thus respond to His love for men in His Incarnation.

IV. The last act of Mary's adoration was, doubtless, an act of tender compassion for poor sinners, for whose salvation the Word became Incarnate. She knew how to use this compassion for their interests; she offered herself to do penance for them, to suffer for them, in order to obtain their pardon and their return to God. She begged for them the happiness of knowing their Creator and their Redeemer; the grace of loving and serving Him, and thus rendering to the Most Holy Trinity the honor and glory which is Their due. O that I could adore our Lord as Mary did, for I possess Him, as she did, in Holy Communion!

O My God, I ask of Thee this day a great favor: give me the Most Blessed Virgin Adoratrix as my own Mother; let me share in her grace, in that state of uninterrupted adoration in which she was during the whole time that she bore Thee in her chaste womb, that paradise of virtue and of love.

I feel, O my God, that this would be one of the greatest graces of my life. I desire henceforth to adore Thee in union with the Mother of adorers, the Queen of the Cenacle.

MARY'S CHASUBLE

Saint Bonnet, Bishop of Clermont, a very devout servant of Jesus and Mary, had, on the Vigil of the Assumption, retired to the Church of St Michael, to pass the night in prayer and so prepare for the great Feast of his beloved Queen. As he poured out his soul in sighs and ardent desires, he heard the sound of sweet melodies, coming as it were from heaven. All at once the church was lit up and its arches echoed as on days of great solemnity when crowds of people filled the aisles. Stupefied, beside himself, the Saint looked about and saw the Most Holy Virgin, surrounded by a troop of angels and virgins, advance in procession to the foot of the altar. The virgins and angels were singing the praises of their Queen, together with those of her Son. The angels then asked who would celebrate the Holy Mysteries, and Mary replied: "It will be my servant Bonnet who is secretly praying in this church." The angels at once went for the frightened Saint, who had hidden himself in the furthest nook of the church. They clothed him in magnificent vestments and assisted him to celebrate Mass in Mary's presence.

The Holy Sacrifice being at an end, the Holy Virgin blessed her servant, and as a token of her visit so full of love, left him the beautiful chasuble brought down from heaven. This miraculous vestment was kept at Clermont up to the Revolution. It was so delicate, so lovely, that it was never possible to ascertain of what material it was made; it was so delicately embroidered that only the fingers of an angel, or rather of the Queen of Angels could have accomplished such work. (*Bolland., 15 January.*)

Practice—Let us make our thanksgiving after Holy Communion very faithfully, in union with Mary.

Aspiration—O Mary, I have received thy well-beloved Son, and I shall never let Him go!

EIGHTH DAY

THE DIGNITY OF THE DIVINE MATERNITY

Mary, Mother of Jesus the Son of God, *Maria de qua natus est Jesus!* Behold the sublime praise that the Gospel bestows on Mary! The Holy Ghost praises neither her gifts nor her virtues. He contents Himself with showing their divine principle, the fittingness of her divine Maternity. Because she was to be the Mother of God she was given all sanctifying grace, all honor. When one calls her "Mother of God," one has said everything.

I. Mary came to raise up the human race, to restore to motherhood that crown of honor and nobility which Eve lost by her sin. Satan had uncrowned our first mother: Mary reinstates her. She comes—typified by all such noble women of the Ancient Law as Judith, Esther, Deborah—as Queen and liberatrix. When the Archangel appeared to Mary he saluted her with profound respect, not daring to pronounce her name: *"Ave, gratia plena!"* Notice the difference between the language of the Archangel to the true Mother of the living, and that of the fallen angel to the unfortunate Eve!

Mary conceived God; she bore in her virginal womb, the Savior of the world, the source of love; bore Him who came to bring peace to men; whilst the first-born of Eve—Cain—is a sinner, a fratricide.

Mary was honored by shepherds and kings, by the poor and the rich. In her capacity of Mother of God she was established as Queen of the entire world. The Son of God honored Mary as His true Mother and fulfilled towards her all the duties of a son, giving us the example of the most perfect fulfillment of the fourth Commandment: "Honor thy father and thy mother."

II. Eve, by her transgression, lost her liberty and her power, *sub potestate viri eris:* "Thou shalt be," said God to her, "under the power of man"; and since then woman has been either the slave of man, or under his guardianship.

Behold the strong woman, "the Mother" *par excellence*. A mother has a right over her son, be he king, or be he God; so Mary commands Jesus, and Jesus, before whom the powers of heaven tremble, obeys Mary! She alone may command Him publicly, claim the right of a Mother over Him: *Fili, quid fecisti nobis sic?* See, then, Mary's authority. It is she who, at Cana, releases the power of Jesus, thus giving Him, in a fashion, His majority.

Crown of authority—this, then, is the second privilege of her Divine Maternity!

III. There was also given to Mary a crown of glory. Eve, because of her sinful ambition, was stripped of all her glory. She was shamefully driven out of Paradise and she brought forth her children in pain and shame.

Mary gave birth to the Savior in joy. She knew not the pain of maternity. The Savior in passing through her womb bequeathed His glory, and Mary will be Queen because she has given to the world Jesus Christ, King. She is Queen of the Angels, Queen of the Church. Kings will lay their empires at her feet; nations will confide to her their safety, and wherever we find a throne erected to Jesus, there we shall find one dedicated to Mary: Mary's altar is always side by side with that of Jesus.

This, then, is the honor, the dignity, and the glory of the Divine Maternity: Mary is honored, powerful and glorious in Jesus and by Jesus. She is His Divine Mother!

THE COUNCIL OF EPHESUS

(431)

There was once a bishop of Constantinople named Nestorius, who dared to say that the Blessed Virgin was not the Mother of God. "She is," said he, "the Mother of Christ; that is, of a man, to whom the Son of God united Himself." He dared to preach this from the pulpit, before the Faithful of Constantinople; but they arose in indignation, declaring that Jesus Christ was not a man, that He was God, and that the Blessed Virgin being His true Mother was the Mother of God, the real Mother of God. They appealed to the Pope, chief of Bishops, and infallible judge in matters of Faith.

Saint Celestin I, who was Pope at that time, summoned a General Council of all the Bishops, to meet in the City of Ephesus, in Asia Minor, in order to condemn the heresy of Nestorius.

The Council of Ephesus was opened with great solemnity in the year 431. In the early morning the people surrounded the Church of Saint Mary, where the Fathers of the Council had just gathered. All clamored for the honor of the Blessed Virgin to be vindicated. Nestorius, although summoned three different times before the Council, refused to appear. The house in which he had shut himself was guarded by a troop of soldiers, lent to him by a certain Count Candidien, the Ambassador of the Emperor.

At last by evening, the doors of the Council were thrown open, St. Cyril, Patriarch of Alexandria, the Pope's Legate, proclaimed the Council's Decree, which declared that the Blessed Virgin was truly the Mother of God; that Nestorius was guilty of blasphemy in saying the contrary; and that from then on he ceased to be Bishop and Patriarch of Constantinople. Immediately the whole city of Ephesus resounded with songs of joy: from every quarter was heard: "Long live Mary the Mother of God." When the Bishops left the church they were triumphantly escorted home by the light of a thousand torches. The air was filled with perfumes which were burned in pans by the women, in honor of the Fathers of the Council. The city was illuminated, and the joy felt by the children of God soon spread throughout the whole world.

As to Nestorius, at first he tried to resist the Pope and the Council, but the Emperor, informed of the truth, abandoned him, and condemned him to exile. He never consented to submit.

He lived eight years more, with rage in his heart and blasphemies on his lips. At last he died miserably, his body being putrified, and his tongue, that tongue which had blasphemed the Blessed Virgin, which had dared to say and to repeat: "If anyone says that Mary is the Mother of God let him be anathema," that tongue was devoured by worms even before he had drawn his last breath. (*Msgr. de Ségur.*)

Practice—We should frequently receive the God of the Eucharist as a remedy against concupiscence, and as a safeguard of innocence.

Aspiration—Hail, Mary! spiritual Paradise of God, in which flourished the spotless and fragrant Lily, Jesus Eucharistic!

NINTH DAY

The Interior Life of Mary

I. Mary adorned with all gifts, enriched with all virtues, incomparable in merit, appeared to the world under a most ordinary exterior. There was nothing brilliant in her actions; her virtues did not seem to be above the average. Her life was passed in silence and obscurity, and the Gospel narrative says nothing about it. This was because Mary was to be an illustrious model of the hidden life—a life hidden in God with Jesus Christ—a life which we should strive to honor and faithfully copy in our conduct. I wish to show that the law of holiness which God follows in our souls, is the very same that He followed in Mary.

The Church sings of Mary: "All the glory of the King's daughter is within." This is the character of Mary's sanctity. Nothing exterior, nothing conspicuous, all for God alone and known only to Him. And yet, Mary was the holiest, the most perfect of creatures. More loved by God than any creature, the Blessed Virgin received from His bounty the richest of His graces, the most excellent of His gifts. The Eternal

Father gave her all her virtues as Mother; the Son, all the graces of Redemption; the Holy Ghost, the grace of love. Yet Mary lived the most commonplace life, quite hidden and unknown. Must we not therefore conclude that the retired, interior life is the most perfect? The exterior life, even when dedicated to God, is less perfect. Thus the life of our Lord was much more hidden from the eyes of men than made manifest. The Saints were formed on His Model. To be a friend of God, one must be ground to powder, reduced to nothing, annihilated as Jesus and Mary were.

II. Hence I say, if we wish to become saints, we must become interior souls. We are obliged thereto by our vocation as adorers. Without this interior spirit, how can we pray? If in the presence of our Lord we cannot spend a single instant without a book, if we have nothing to say to Him from our own heart, what are we going to do at adoration? What! can we never speak to Him from the abundance of our own heart? Must we always borrow the thoughts and words of strangers? No, no! Let us strive to become recollected, interior souls. No one can be this in the way that Jesus and Mary were; but every one can become recollected in the degree given him by grace. Without the interior life, we shall never receive any consolation, encouragement in prayer; we shall only be unhappy at the feet of our Lord. If we wish to become true adorers, we must have this interior spirit. We should talk to our Lord when kneeling in His presence, ask Him questions, await His reply: we should enjoy God's presence. We should be happy in His company, happy in His service; we should take pleasure in His familiarity, so sweet, so encouraging. But to discover the Heart of Jesus we must be interior. After all, what does it mean to be interior? It means to love, to converse, to live with Jesus. But Jesus does not make Himself heard by bodily ears, nor seen with bodily eyes; He speaks only to the recollected soul. He is wholly interior in the Blessed Sacrament: He no longer enters into the heart through the sight, as during His mortal life; He now enters the soul direct, and speaks to it alone. When the soul does not expand in His presence it is because He does not act upon it— there is some obstacle in His path.

Ah! do not make our Lord out to have said what is not true! He has said that His yoke is sweet and His burden light. But it is only so for him who carries it in a prayerful, recollected spirit; otherwise, he will find it heavy and fatiguing. When we do not lead interior lives, everything we do goes haltingly. Oh, how I should wish to see accomplished in us what was so fully realized in the Blessed Virgin: "The kingdom of God is within you"—the kingdom of love, of virtue, and of interior graces! Then indeed should we begin to be adorers and saints. The grass of the field dies yearly, because its roots do not lie deep in the soil; but the oak, the olive, and the cedar stand, year after year, because their roots run deep into the earth. In order to grow strong, to endure, we must descend to the very depths, even to self-annihilation. There we shall find Jesus. He is there, annihilated: *exinanivit*. It was thus that Mary found him. Oh, may that Blessed Mother, our perfect exemplar of the interior life, make us live, as she did, in Jesus! May we, like her, remain always in Him and never leave Him!

BLESSED PETER JULIAN EYMARD

Blessed Peter Eymard was chosen by Divine Providence to be the Founder of two religious Orders in the Church: one for priests, and the other for nuns, both entirely consecrated to the adoration of the Most Blessed Sacrament *exposed*. But it was through Mary that God made His will known to His servant; so is it declared in the Brief of Beatification: "On the Feast of Corpus Christi of the year 1845, moved by an inspiration which we may look upon as divine, he clearly understood the nature of the work that he was soon to undertake to promote the worship of the Most Blessed Sacrament. Nevertheless, it was not until the Most Blessed Virgin (whose help and light he had previously implored in the sanctuary of Fourvière) gave him two forewarnings, that, humbly submitting to the will of God, he began to lay the foundation of his new Order."

The first of these warnings took place on January 21, 1851. Blessed Eymard, while in Mary's sanctuary, was strongly impressed by the thought of the small amount of devotion that existed towards the Blessed Sacrament, and of the sacrileges committed against the Divine Eucharist. A few days later, the 2nd of February, this idea became more distinct. The Father was to preside at the meeting of the Third Order of Mary; he was going to Fourvière by the "ascent of angels." "I remember," he used to relate, "that I did not want to go into the sanctuary, from a feeling of humility, and I took my place beyond the pulpit. There I asked Mary what I could do to make the Most Blessed Sacrament loved. I said to her: 'Each Order honors some mystery: the Eucharist, the greatest of all, is the only one that has none!' Then Mary told me she wanted me to devote myself to having her Divine Son honored in the Eucharist. It was there that Mary was so good to me. I saw clearly what she asked of me."

Yes, it was through Mary that Blessed Peter Eymard was led to Jesus. He wrote on this subject in his notes during a retreat in 1865. "It was the Blessed Virgin who led me to our Lord: to Sunday Communion (at Notre Dame du Laus) at the age of twelve; from the Society of Mary to that of the Most Blessed Sacrament."

Practice—Let us strive to live in recollection and in union with Jesus present in us, in imitation of our Mother.

Aspiration—O Mary, true daughter of the King, all thy glory is in thy interior, because Jesus dwells therein.

Pray For Me

✠

Of ties of friendship here on earth
  No stronger, sweeter can there be
Than those expressed in grief or mirth
  In these brief words, "Friend, pray for me."

May God's choice blessings on thee rest
  And keep thy soul from evil free,
May angels guard thee and request
  That thou should'st often pray for me.

Amid the changing scenes of life,
  Whate'er thy future lot may be,
In smiles or tears, in peace or strife,
  Where'er thou art, oh, pray for me.

And when beneath the verdant sod
  My earthly form in death shall be,
Then recommend my soul to God
  And o'er my grave, oh, pray for me.

To Hilda with a blessing and deepest gratitude for great kindnesses. May God in His goodness always bless, guide and protect you.

Begging your prayers and sharing in mine

Yours faithfully in Christ

Louis A. Wheeler

S J

TENTH DAY

Modesty, a Characteristic of Mary's Life

Mary's hidden life possesses a characteristic that distinguishes it from that of Jesus. We do not find in Mary that humility which astonishes and confounds, that admixture of power and weakness, of dignity and of submission, which is so admirable in the life of Jesus. Mary's life is always the same, simple and hidden, profoundly humble and modest. Modesty was a characteristic of her piety, of her virtues, and of all her actions.

I. Mary was modest in her exterior. She was distinguished neither by an austere demeanor nor by an affected carelessness. Humble and sweet, like unto her Divine Son, her whole exterior bespoke her lowly condition and made her seem like a woman of the people. We, too, should try to avoid attracting attention to ourselves, by modesty of behavior, if we wish to resemble our Blessed Mother in her life.

II. Mary was modest in the world. She eagerly sacrificed her privacy and the sweetness of heavenly contemplation in order to go to her cousin Elizabeth, to congratulate her and to render her assistance. For three months, she was her constant companion, humbly waiting upon her; and she was the delight of that privileged household. When her Son's glory demanded it, Mary appeared in public. She was present at the wedding feast of Cana. She spoke no word in her own praise, nor did she bring forward her title of Mother of God, nor the power and glory of her Son in order to gain the esteem of men. In her modesty, she gave heed to the call of charity and withdrew when she was no longer needed.

III. Mary was modest in her duties. She fulfilled them all with sweetness, without eagerness, always satisfied, always prepared to take up some new duty. She fulfilled them with that equability of character which never lets any difficulty be seen and never asks for consolation, that never attracts attention, because everything is done simply and as a matter of course. She is therefore a beautiful model for all those who wish to live the life of Jesus Eucharistic. The life of an adorer, consecrated to the service of the Eucharistic King, is composed of little sacrifices which God alone sees and rewards. The lowliness of his service constitutes all the honor, all the joy of his filial devotedness, and his sole ambition is to please his Master by the constant sacrifice of self.

IV. Mary was modest in her piety.

Mary, elevated to the highest degree of prayer to which any creature can attain, lived in the habitual exercise of perfect love, exalted above all the Angels, and forming by her dignity of Mother of God an order apart in the wonders of God. She served her Lord, nevertheless, in the common, ordinary way of piety. She followed the prescriptions of the Law, assisted at the legal feasts, prayed with the multitude. Nothing distinguished her, not even her modesty, which she kept concealed. Nothing, not even extraordinary fervor, revealed in her exterior the perfection of her piety.

Such ought to be our piety; nothing conspicuous in its practices, simple and modest in its action, carefully shunning all singularity (the subtle fruit of self-love) and everything out of the ordinary, as likely to lead to vanity and illusion.

V. Mary was modest in her virtues. Mary possessed all virtues in a supreme degree, and practiced them all in their sovereign perfection, but not in an extraordinary manner. Her humility saw only the goodness of God, and for all the favors that she had received, she showed only humble gratitude, the gratitude of the poor—silent and undemonstrative, unnoticed by the world. "Can anything good come from Nazareth?" Consequently no attention was paid to Mary.

Behold the great secret of perfection: to

know how to find it in what is most simple; to know how to nourish it in what is most common; to know how to preserve it in the midst of indifference and forgetfulness. Virtue that is paraded in public is in a perilous condition; virtue that is lauded and extolled is very near a fall. The flower that every one admires, quickly fades.

Let us, then, love the little virtues of Nazareth, those hidden virtues that are born at the foot of the Cross, under the shadow of Jesus and Mary; then shall we fear neither the tempest that shatters the cedars, nor the thunderbolt that strikes the mountain top.

VI. Mary was modest in her sacrifices. Mary accepted exile silently and sweetly without a word of repining. She did not esteem herself the more because she was destined for great sacrifices, nor did she complain or beg for a lessening of their rigor.

She was modest in enduring the anguish of her holy spouse. Rather than speak to him of the great mystery operated in her, which would have exalted her so in his eyes, she submitted to his doubts in silence and waited for Heaven to vindicate her virtue, calmly abandoning herself to Divine Providence.

With her heart pierced with sorrow, Mary followed her Son bearing His Cross; but she did not fill the streets of Jerusalem with her cries and her wails. On Calvary, plunged in an immeasurable sorrow, a sorrow as deep as her love, Mary suffered in silence; and after having taken a silent farewell of her Son, she withdrew—brokenhearted, but resigned.

VII. Finally, Mary was modest in her glory, and this is the most wonderful triumph of Mary's modesty.

Mary by reason of her remarkable dignity as Mother of God has the right to the homage of the universe; yet Mary retained only the anguish and the sacrifice of her motherhood. Never was she seen in public when Her Son was honored and acclaimed, but when there was humiliation, or suffering to be shared with Him, His Mother was always to be found by His side.

If, then, we desire to be true children of this loving Mother, we must clothe ourselves with her modesty. Let us often make this virtue the subject of our meditation, for it is the heritage left us by Mary. Let her modesty be the rule of our conduct. Let her simplicity, which forgets itself, seeing God alone, which inclines her towards duty rather than pleasure, to God Himself rather than to His consolation, to love for love's sake—let this single-mindedness, then, be our portion, the aim of all our efforts and the characteristic of our life.

Modesty is the sovereign virtue of an adorer, since it is the virtue of the servants of kings, and the virtue of the Angels in presence of the Divine Majesty.

Modesty should, therefore, regulate our demeanor in the presence of God, when we offer Him the homage of our senses and of our faculties. It is the etiquette of His royal service. We must be modest even as Mary, in the service of Jesus!

THE ANGEL OF THE EUCHARIST

It is well known by what devoted love and tender fidelity to the Eucharist a poor working girl, Marie Eustelle, merited the beautiful name of "the Angel of the Eucharist."

Being appointed by her pastor to take care of the parish sacristy, it is impossible to relate with what reverence and devotion she performed this sacred function, treated, alas! in some parishes with so little respect—by hirelings.

The first time it fell to her lot to prepare what was necessary for the offering of the Holy Sacrifice, the joy of her soul was equaled only by the deep sense of her unworthiness. She wrote on this subject: "I love to think that like the Blessed Virgin I am employed in the service of the Temple as much as my avocation will permit; and this thought rekindles my gratitude. But to be worthy of this holy position I would need the purity of the Holy Virgin, which I am very far from having. O my God! I do not think enough about the account I must give in return for all these means of salvation. I am only taken up with the happiness this holy occupation brings me. May the Lord deign to adorn my soul with the purity of the Angels, in order to draw so near to the Lord of the Angels, and to receive Him so often!" (*Vie de Marie Eustelle.*)

Practice—Let us try to show in our life the modesty of Jesus and His holy Mother.

Aspiration—We bless thee, O chaste Dove, who didst bring to us the olive branch, and who didst predict Jesus Hostia, who will save us from spiritual deluge.

ELEVENTH DAY

Mary at Bethlehem

The mystery of Bethlehem is full of love and sweetness. Jesus appears here, if one may say so, more pleasing than upon Calvary. Let us enter into the attitude of mind of the Most Blessed Virgin.

I. Let us unite with Mary in her expectation, during the hours that preceded the blessed moment of her Son's birth. Like her, let us redouble our love and fervor and unite ourselves with her recollection. And let her habit of life teach us this lesson: to serve our Lord as He wishes us to serve Him, and not to seek to please ourselves in His service.

Mary knew from the Prophecies all the suffering that awaited her Son, and she was ready to serve Him in His way, and to follow Him everywhere. Let us imitate this spirit of self-sacrifice, this true love.

It would have seemed perfectly natural to Mary for Jesus to have been born in a beautiful palace, or at least in some degree of comfort. But no, He was born in a cave, in the hole of a rock, into which, after having been everywhere repulsed, Mary and

Joseph were forced to retire. St Joseph's sorrow must indeed have been very great! It was incumbent on him as head of the family to find shelter for his holy spouse, and we can well imagine what must have been his anxiety, his distress, when, denied admittance everywhere, he was forced to lead Mary, about to bring forth her Child, to this wretched hole. But Mary was happy even in the midst of these rebuffs. She possessed Jesus in her bosom and she knew that it was He who permitted that they should be rejected and despised, He who had led them to that stable in which He had willed to be born.

Thus it is that God accomplishes His ends. Man is disturbed; he seeks human helps, and when he has exhausted all known means in vain, God leads him where He wills. God permits that we often vainly seek the help of men, in order that we may abandon ourselves more fully to Him and allow ourselves to be led, even as Mary and Joseph. It is in this state of abandonment that we feel most sensibly the goodness of God. He then takes care of us, and we confidently draw near to Him, as children around their Father. When success crowns our efforts, when Divine Providence has shown Himself more sensibly to us, our love is no longer the same, for we, perhaps, then count too much on our own efforts and not enough on God. The Israelites received more favors in the desert than in the Promised Land, and God was nearer to them there; Jesus was more approachable in His crib at Bethlehem or in the lowly house of Nazareth, than in His public life, in the midst of all the wonders that He wrought.

II. And when Jesus is born, Oh! let us realize if we can, the adoration, the homage, the attentions of Mary. Let us adore Jesus in her arms, or sleeping on her breast. What a beautiful ostensorium! It has been wrought with all the skill of the Holy Spirit. Who, indeed, could be more beautiful than Mary, even exteriorly? She is that pure lily of the valley that has grown in an immaculate soil. Mary is the paradise of God! And see this other flower that has blossomed there—Jesus, the Flower of Jesse! See what the harvest has brought forth—Jesus, the Wheat of the elect! Let us now penetrate into Mary's soul and contemplate its beauty. There is beauty enough there to give us unending happiness when we come to know it well. Almighty God has exhausted His power, so to say, in embellishing Mary. She becomes the ostensorium of the Word Incarnate. She is the channel by which Jesus comes to us!

Ah, yes! The Eucharist began at Bethlehem in Mary's arms. It was she who brought to humanity the Bread for which it was famishing, and which alone can nourish it. She it was who took care of that Bread for us. It was she who nourished the Lamb whose life-giving Flesh we feed upon. She nourished Him with her virginal milk; she nourished Him for the sacrifice, for she foreknew His destiny. Yes, she knew from the beginning, and every day she realizes it more fully, that her Lamb is only for immolation. She accepts God's will, and, bearing Him in her arms, herself prepares for us the Victim of Calvary—that Victim of our Altars. On the day of the Sacrifice she herself will conduct her Divine Lamb to Jerusalem, to deliver Him up to Divine Justice for the world's salvation. Ah, Bethlehem already speaks of Calvary! Truly had Mary heard her Son's first word: "Father, sacrifice and oblation Thou wouldst not. . . . Behold, I come!" and she united herself in His offering and His anticipated immolation.

III. But Bethlehem had its joys also, joys most sweet and consoling. The shepherds—simple souls—came to adore the Infant Savior. Mary rejoiced at seeing their homage and the willing offerings they made to her Jesus.

Some days later it is the Magi who bring their tribute of adoration and their royal gifts. Mary offers her Babe to their love; it is in her arms that they find Him.

O how often may we not share in the

happiness of the Magi! How happy is the loving soul when it has found Jesus with Mary, His Mother! They who know the Tabernacle where He dwells, they who receive Him into their souls, know that His conversation is full of divine sweetness, His consolation ravishing, His peace superabundant, and the familiarity of His love and His Heart ineffable.

To find Jesus in the arms of His Mother, to unite oneself to Mary's sentiments as she presses Him to her heart—O what a ravishing moment! Like the joy of Thabor, it passes all too quickly! Oh, wonderful moment in which all else is forgotten, in which we no longer desire anything else, not even heaven—for we possess it already, we have Jesus and Mary.

CHURCHES FOR THE EUCHARIST ARE MULTIPLIED THROUGH MARY'S SOLICITUDE

If the Blessed Virgin inspires so many of her devout servants to make pilgrimages and build temples in her honor, let us not doubt that she does it to multiply the Tabernacles of her Son, the God of the Eucharist. Of this we have a precious witness in the erection of the Chapel of Our Lady of Laus, situated in the Alps. Addressing herself to a pious shepherdess whom she wished to make the instrument of her graces, Mary said: "I want to have a church built here in honor of my very dear Son; where many sinners will come to be converted."

The church was built with the mite given by the

ELEVENTH DAY

poor, and Mary once more addressing the same child, said: "My Son has given me this spot for the conversion of sinners." And the history of Laus bears witness, that never did a sinner leave this blessed sanctuary without being reconciled with the Divine Son of the most sweet Mother, who was waiting for him in His Tabernacle, the throne of mercy and grace. *(Histoire des merveilles de Notre-Dame-du-Laus.)*

Practice—Let us constantly ask Mary to give us Jesus.

Aspiration—Hail, Mary, holy mountain upon which the Eucharistic Lamb found rich pasturage!

TWELFTH DAY

Jesus Presented in the Temple by Mary

I. Our Lord did not wish to delay His offering of Himself publicly to His Father. Forty days after His birth, He inspires Mary to take Him to the Temple. Mary carries her Infant in her arms; she is going to offer Him to His Father, and then redeem Him with two turtle-doves, for Jesus willed to be bought back with these little creatures typifying His purity and simplicity. A great mystery took place there.

The joy, the bliss of the Most Blessed Virgin Mary came to an end on that day. Listen to the words of this aged man, this chosen one of God: "This child is set for the fall and for the resurrection of many in Israel; . . . and thy own soul a sword shall pierce."

How can the Holy Trinity, how can God, so good, so tender, thus reveal such a mystery of sorrow to this poor young mother of fifteen, who is still overwhelmed with joy at the birth of her Son? It is her first visit to the Temple since His birth, and she is told of the cruel death awaiting her beloved Child. Ah! well does she understand!

From that day, Calvary is wherever Jesus is; at Nazareth, in Egypt—everywhere does she behold her Jesus crucified. When our soul is not strong in virtue, God lets us live a more or less shielded life: but when He sees a really loving soul, He hastens to crucify it in order to show forth His glory therein. Love entails suffering. Mary accepts everything. Henceforth she converses with her Son but of Calvary, of His sufferings and death. She must indeed have fortitude to endure a Calvary that is to last thirty-three years! "Thy own soul a sword shall pierce." Do we understand the crucifixion implied in these words? From then on, Mary sees her Son's sufferings in every detail. She thinks of them incessantly. From that moment she became the Queen of Martyrs.

II. What must we glean from the mystery of the Presentation of Jesus by Mary? The lesson is this: we must not give ourselves to God's service in order to enjoy consolation, to possess unalterable peace and tranquillity. Jesus does indeed say: "My yoke is sweet and my burden is light"; but He has also said: "He that does not take up his cross daily and follow Me is not worthy of Me."

What, then, should we do? We should offer ourselves in union with Mary, our Mother, give ourselves unreservedly to God, and accept the pain, the suffering and the crosses that He may will to send us. In the beginning, when the soul first gives itself to God, it often experiences great consolation; the service of God seems to be full of sensible sweetness. There are many souls who, disgusted with the world and its deceits, return to a life of piety to find peace and consolation. They seek that alone; they desire to find only that in God's service. They serve Him as long as He bestows upon them His divine favors; but when He hides Himself and wishes to substitute stronger nourishment for children's food, they become disgusted, discouraged and scrupulous. They torture their imaginations to find out what could have drawn upon them such punishment. They fancy that their confessions have not been sincere, that they have made bad Communions. They seek to find in themselves the cause of the change. When they do not succeed, they become despondent and usually end by abandoning their pious exercises.

We must not, of course, disdain God's consolations, we must receive them joyfully when He sends them; but we must not seek them alone. Such sweetness, such favors pass, while Jesus alone remaineth forever. There have been saints who were favored with great consolations from God, with ecstasies—but oh, how they suffered! God gave them these favors only at rare intervals; they were the recompense of their sufferings and an encouragement to suffer still more for His love. It is by suffering that we are sanctified, by crosses and trials that the soul is strengthened, freed from self, in order that it may find its satisfaction in God, and God alone.

This is the lesson of the mystery of Mary's Purification, and of Jesus' Presentation in the Temple. Let us put it into practice if we wish to be worthy of the August Victim, whom we incessantly contemplate in the Blessed Sacrament, and of His Mother who so generously offered Him for us.

THE MIRACULOUS DEDICATION OF THE SANCTUARY OF OUR LADY OF THE HERMITS

In September 948, the Abbé Eberhard of Einsiedeln begged St Conrad, Bishop of Constance, to whose diocese Einsiedeln belonged, to come and consecrate the church. The prelate arrived September 13th, accompanied by Ulric, the holy Bishop of Augsburg, and a number of noblemen. The 14th being the day appointed for the ceremony, Conrad, with a few religious, went down towards the middle of the night into the church and began to pray. Suddenly the chapel was illuminated by a celestial light, and they saw Jesus Christ Himself at the altar celebrating the office of Dedication, assisted by the four Evangelists. Angels poured perfumes everywhere about the Divine Pontiff. The Apostle St Peter and Pope St

Gregory held the pontifical insignia; the Holy Mother of God stood before the altar enveloped in a halo of glory. The arches resounded with celestial hymns chanted by an angelic choir, led by St Michael the Archangel. St Stephen and St Lawrence, the most illustrious martyred deacons, fulfilled the functions of their Order. St Conrad himself in some of his writings alludes to various alterations made by the angelic voices in the singing of the *Sanctus,* the *Agnus Dei,* and the last *Dominus Vobiscum.* In one of these they sang: "Have pity on us, O Lord, whose holiness shines forth in the sanctuary of the glorious Virgin. Blessed by Mary's Son, who comes here to reign forever." The Bishop, notwithstanding his surprise at such an apparition, continued in prayer until the eleventh hour of the day. They waited for him, without daring, however, to inquire into the cause of his delay.

Finally some of the brothers requested him to begin the ceremony. Conrad, without moving, related with simplicity what he had seen and heard. They thought, however, that he was still under the influence of a dream. At last the holy Bishop, yielding to the solicitations of all, began the consecration. It was then that an unknown voice, which filled the vast enclosure, fell upon the astonished ears of the beholders, repeating in the language of the Church: *"Cessa, cessa, frater! Capella divinitus consecrata est."* "Cease, cease, my Brother, the chapel has been Divinely consecrated!"

Sixteen years later, St Conrad, St Ulric, and other eye witnesses of this event, being gathered together in Rome, solemnly vouched for it. After making all necessary judicial inquiries, Leo VIII issued a Bull concerning this case, in order to give it greater publicity. This Bull was ratified by the following Popes: Innocent IV, Martin V, Nicholas IV, Eugène IV, Nicholas V, Pius II, Jules II,

Leo X, Pius IV, Gregory XIII, Clement VII and Urban VIII.

Finally on Mary 15, 1793, Pius VI ratified the acts of his predecessors, in spite of the skeptics, always ready to doubt what they do not care to accept, and ever ready to put faith in absurd beliefs which please them. *(Description du couvent et de l'abbaye d'Einsiedeln.)*

Practice—We should offer ourselves to Jesus, the Victim of love on our Altars, and accept all that He may wish to send us, in union with Mary.

Aspiration—O Mary, fruitful Vine that hast given us the Eucharistic Wine, be thou forever blessed!

THIRTEENTH DAY

The Life of the Holy Family

Let us meditate upon the life of the Holy Family, the life of Mary and of Joseph in Jesus.

I. Jesus was the center of Mary's and Joseph's love. . . . "Where thy treasure is, there is thy heart." So to possess Jesus was the sole joy of these happy parents. He was their all. They held neither to Bethlehem, nor to Egypt, nor to Nazareth; Jesus was the home of their hearts.

After an enforced absence from that humble home, how quickly St Joseph returns! With what joy, what happiness does he approach the house where dwells Jesus, the Divine Child. He does not waste any time away from Him! He knows Jesus is Divine Love Incarnate.

In the same way, my house, my family, my center is the Eucharist, the Tabernacle near which I dwell. Like Mary and Joseph I should feel at home only there.

II. Jesus was the end of Mary's and Joseph's existence; they lived only for Him; they labored for Him alone. O how gladly did St Joseph labor to gain for Him and His

Divine Mother their daily bread! With what great satisfaction he brought home the meager pittance received for his work! And when his menial task was more than usually laborious, how sweet that fatigue was to him, since it was all for Jesus!

And for us, too, Jesus Eucharistic should be the Object of our life, our joy—the inspiration of our work. What life could be more beautiful than that which is passed in the company of Jesus in the Most Blessed Sacrament!

III. Jesus was the constant nourishment of Mary's and Joseph's life of union and love. They found their delight in gazing at Him, listening to Him, in admiring His obedience, in watching Him at His work and at prayer, for "He did all things well."

But, above all, they were happy in studying His intentions, in acquainting themselves with His sentiments, the motive of His virtues. They beheld Him incessantly seeking after and selecting, by preference, occasions of poverty, obedience and penance. They contemplated His humility and self-annihilation, while they admired His fidelity in referring all to the glory of His father, never desiring, like mankind, to be the object of any praise, any glory.

Jesus, Mary and Joseph had but one aim in life, they wished but for one thing, the honor and glory of the Heavenly Father.

This should be my ambition; but in order to accomplish this, I must unite myself with Mary and Jesus. I must share their life, their family life, that intimate life of which God alone holds the secret.

O how happy is the soul in contemplating the hidden life of the Holy Family, all that is said and done therein—the Gospel of the family of Jesus! What wonderful evenings they must have had together at Nazareth! What heavenly conversations, what prayers! Assuredly Jesus must have explained to Mary and Joseph all that the Scriptures have said concerning Him. We will listen while He reveals Calvary to them, tells them of all the humiliation and suffering through which He has to pass. He shows them in His hands the places where the nails are to be driven; and this in order that Calvary may even now begin to bear fruit in the soul of His Mother and His holy guardian. He speaks to them of the Church, of the Apostles, of the Religious Orders which will consecrate themselves to His, and to their, honor. He speaks to them of us, of our miseries, and of the immense love that He bears us.

Nazareth has become a heaven of love, the paradise of the second Adam and the new Eve; a heaven of the purest virtues, of the holiest love. What a delicious perfume ascended to the Lord from that delectable garden in which blossomed the Incarnate Word, Mary, and Joseph the Just! The Heavenly Father found therein His delight; the angelic spirits looked upon it in admiration. As for me, I desire to glean from it love for a pious and recollected life in Jesus, Mary and Joseph.

THE TWO GUARDIANS OF THE VIRGIN

God from all eternity having ordained the course of Mary's life, elected two men destined successively to become the guardians of that incomparable Virgin; and the mission He reserved for them being a most sublime one, He called them both to an eminent, and even exceptional, degree of sanctity. What traits of resemblance existed between the two men? Being called to live in close intimacy with a Virgin, it was fitting they should both be resplendent: this is why they were both adorned with the virtue of virginity.

One sums up in himself the most brilliant glories of the ancient Covenant; he inherits the dignity of the Patriarchs; he is the possessor of all the good things promised by the Prophets. The other obtains the most august dignities of the new Covenant; he is an Apostle; he is a Pontiff; he will be an Evangelist, a prophet and a martyr.

In the one we honor the true Spouse of the Virgin; in the other, her son through grace.

The one is Mary's guardian before and while she possesses Jesus; the other is her guardian when Jesus is taken from her.

It is given to the one to press the Son of Man to his heart; it is given to the other to lean on the Heart of the Son of Man.

The one nourishes Jesus by the fruit of his labors; the other is nourished with Jesus at the

Last Supper, where he drank of Love from the fountain head.

The one faithfully accompanies Jesus and Mary when the mysteries begin; he is in the Temple beside the Priest and the Virgin during the oblation of the great Victim; the other, no less faithful, accompanies Jesus and Mary when the mysteries are nearing their end, he is before the altar of the Cross, near this same Priest and this same Virgin during the consummation of the Sacrifice.

Incomparable men to whom God confided His most precious treasures. Their hands were worthy to touch the Word of Life and to serve His Holy Mother; this is why every age touched with admiration will honor their virtue, and sing their happiness. (Msgr. Van den Berghe, *Marie et le Sacerdoce.*)

Practice—Let us always conduct ourselves with ceremonial respect when in the presence of the Blessed Sacrament.

Aspiration—O Mary, thou who so perfectly served Jesus Eucharistic, vouchsafe to be our instructress in this divine art.

FOURTEENTH DAY

Mary's Compassion

I. Mary had neither original nor actual sin to expiate. She had not been charged by God, as Jesus had been, with the weight of our iniquities. How was it, then, that she, the sinless one, should have to suffer so much all her life, during which the vision of her Son's death never ceased to haunt her until it was materialized on Calvary?

The reason is: first, that suffering is the law of love; it was Mary's love that made her martyrdom, and because she loved more than any other creature, she suffered an incomparable martyrdom. Secondly, because suffering is the actual glorification of Jesus Christ in us. By suffering, we continue and complete His Sacrifice. Finally, because maternity is purchased by suffering. In bringing into the world her Spotless Son, Mary escaped that law; but when she was to become our Mother, to bring us forth to grace, she had to feel all its rigor. What did Jesus Christ not suffer in order to create us anew in Himself? Mary, also, as she stands at the foot of the Cross, undergoes all the torments of the Passion, in order to become our Mother by adoption.

Let us, then, reflect upon Mary's share in the Passion of Jesus, and try to understand the part she took in it.

II. By a supernatural light, Mary saw Jesus in the Garden of Olives; she shared in His prayer, His sorrow, His agony, for there was perfect love and sympathy between those two hearts.

Later she saw Jesus betrayed by Judas, abandoned by all, denied by Peter, alone before His judges, without a single defender, ignominiously buffeted, treated as a fool. Alas, poor Mother! how cruel that absolute abandonment must have been to her! What! is there not one—not even among His friends—who will take up His defense! Will no one dare even to recognize Him!

And when St John comes to tell her of the scenes in Pilate's judgment-hall, the iniquitous condemnation to death, her maternal heart must have broken with grief. She arrives at the pretorium: she hears the strokes of the scourging; she sees Jesus placed beside Barabbas and presented to the populace as the equal of that notorious malefactor; she hears the *Ecce Homo,* and the ferocious cries of the impious multitude: "*Tolle, tolle, crucifige!*" "Let Him be crucified, let Him be crucified." Ah, poor Mother, would that she were able to snatch

Him from those cruel executioners! Alas! she has but her tears!

III. She follows Him to Calvary. She meets Him on that way of sorrows which He saturates with His blood. Their eyes meet; their hearts, their sorrow unite in one act of sacrifice, one act of perfect resignation.

Behold Jesus on Calvary! Mary sees Him inhumanly and cruelly despoiled of His garments. She sees Him extended on the Cross; she hears the blows of the hammer that fasten His hands and feet to the gibbet. What a sight for a mother! She, too, is being crucified—the rebounds of the hammer give Mary her stigmata.

She sees Him when they raise Him up from the ground; she follows Him with her eyes. Hardly has the Cross been planted in the ground when that courageous Mother, braving all obstacles, comes close up to the foot of the Cross of her Jesus. There, plunged in the ocean of her grief, she contemplates Him. She herself feels each one of His pains; her heart is congealed by the cries of Jesus. She listens to each of her Son's words; she stores them in her memory in order to retell them to us. She sees His sacred Blood flow down; sees His life draining out of Him. She hears Jesus complain of thirst without being able to assuage it—she, His Mother! And, finally, she hears Jesus cry out that He has been forsaken by His Heavenly Father!—her well-beloved Son has breathed His last sigh.

What does Mary do now? She is in an agony of grief and love, but she receives His sacred Body into her arms, embraces It with a mother's tenderness, adores It with the faith of a Christian, and prepares It for burial as a desolate widow her only son—and then she weeps.

Mary's life will now be passed in recalling the sorrows of the Passion, in order to renew her own martyrdom and the glory rendered to God by her sufferings. She will retrace again and again that path of sorrow, and so be the first to teach us the pious devotion—so powerful with Jesus, and so useful to the soul—The Way of the Cross.

THE PERPETUAL CALVARY

Mary wept and suffered at the foot of the Cross. What must her feeling of sorrow be when she sees her Son still outraged, and treated on our altars with even more contempt than on Calvary?

Sister Mary of the Crucifix, of Palma in Sicily, heard a trumpet blast like thunder sound forth at the moment when a sacrilegious priest was about to say Mass, and these words were heard: *"Ultio, poena, dolor!"* "Vengeance, chastisement, torture!" And she beheld an angel with sword in hand ready to smite the wretch. When he pronounced the words of Consecration, it seemed to her that Jesus, meek as a lamb, allowed Himself to be torn to pieces by this cruel wolf. But when

FOURTEENTH DAY

he came to the Communion the heavens became darkened, the angels around the altar wept; and the Blessed Mother stood near her Son weeping also, and lost in the depths of the unfathomable sorrow caused by the death of her most innocent Jesus, as well as by the loss of this ungrateful son who dared to sacrifice Him in so cruel a manner. (St Alphonsus de' Liguori, *Selva.*)

Practice—In union with Mary, let us repair by all possible means the sacrileges committed against the Blessed Eucharist.

Aspiration.—O Mother of love! grant that we may feel the immensity of thy grief at the sight of Jesus outraged in the Blessed Sacrament.

FIFTEENTH DAY

Mary After the Resurrection

I. As Mary had suffered in union with her Son dying upon the Cross, so did she share in His joy and happiness after His Resurrection; the life of Mary always conformed to the life of Jesus and faithfully reflected it.

For whom was the first visit of the Risen Lord? Assuredly it must have been for His Mother! It would be only just that she having shared in the Sacrifice of His death more completely than any one else should have the first news, the first grace, the first joy of His Resurrection! Therefore He would have gone to her immediately on coming forth from the tomb, glorified and triumphant. He had parted from her in tears, He returns to her with joy! What a moment for Mary, when her Risen Jesus embraces her with all the love and respect that she merited!

What passed between them in that happy meeting? Holy Scripture does not tell us; but we can imagine the beauty of it all. What a glorious reception the Son must have received in His Mother's little room!

Only through love's insight can we reconstruct that scene. Without doubt, Jesus appeared to His Mother in all His Risen beauty. No one of the Apostles could have seen the beauty of Jesus as Mary saw it; spiritual vision is always proportionate to the soul's sanctity, and so Mary penetrated even to His interior glory. She must have seen Him in all the radiant splendor of His Divinity in that blissful moment, since theologians state that she was at times raised up to see God face to face. Our Lord converses with her; He shows her His nail-pierced limbs, those wounds she had so tenderly kissed at the descent from the Cross. But now they are radiant; waves of light issue from those nail wounds in the sacred hands and feet. Even as His members had suffered, so are they now glorified! Mary must have kissed those Sacred Wounds in transports of joy and felt the influx of grace that flowed from them! She must have seen the Sacred Heart of her Son through the pierced side. Now He shows It to her, beating, palpitating with life and darting forth flames of love. Ah! we can easily imagine with what love and tenderness Mary pressed her pure lips to that Sacred Side. And if St John, laying his head upon that Divine Heart hidden in our Lord's earthly body drew from It so many graces, what must it not have been for Mary, when she embraced It, kissed It, uncovered and palpitating under her lips! Then it was that she understood more perfectly still that suffering and glory, death and life are intimately connected in the Divine plan.

II. But our Lord did not come to visit Mary alone: He was accompanied by a retinue of all those Saints who had risen with Him—from the Patriarchs down to St Joseph and the Good Thief. All came in the train of their triumphant King to salute their Queen. Adam and Eve, to whom God had promised this daughter, this Mother of the Savior Messiah, must have prostrated themselves at her feet. It was to her, after our Lord, that they owed their pardon, for it was she who had given them their Liberator. And to all the felicitations of the Saints of the Old Law, who thanked her for having given them a Savior, Mary replied, without doubt, *"Magnificat"*—"My soul doth magnify the Lord, . . . because He hath regarded the humility of His handmaid." And St Joseph, St Joachim and St Ann, did they not also come to pay their visit of respect and love? The sight of the Blessed Virgin must indeed have filled the Saints with joy, so pure a reflex of Jesus' light.

So our Lord leaves His Mother not only consoled, but in an ecstasy of bliss when He goes to show Himself to Mary Magdalen and His Apostles. No doubt but what He came often to see Mary again before His Ascension, to go over with her all the events —both the joys and the sufferings—of His life on earth.

III. From the silence of the Evangelists concerning this apparition, as well as concerning all the other events of our Lady's life, we may draw precious instruction. After having given Jesus to the world Mary was bound to be eclipsed; she had to remain in the background in order to become the model of interior souls, the patroness of the lowly, hidden life. Mary's mission after her Son's Resurrection was one of love and prayer. Our Lord seems to have kept for Himself alone the secret of His Mother's life; He wished it to be entirely for Himself.

There is also another reason. Jesus conceals Himself in the Blessed Sacrament, He veils Himself even more now than during His mortal life: Mary had to imitate that state, share that annihiliation. The hidden life is the more perfect. As Jesus deprived Himself of speech, movement and sensible action in the Eucharist, Mary was no more to speak, no more to appear in the world. Because Jesus had to become a silent Prisoner, Mary devoted herself to guard Him in the privacy of a life entirely devoted to prayer. Had Mary not consecrated herself to this state, we adorers of the Eucharist could never have found in her our model. But Mary, the unknown servant and custodian of the Holy Eucharist, is our Mother and her life is our grace.

As the light and heat of the sun increase until it reaches its meridian, so Mary became more perfect each day. Her last years were filled with a love of whose breadth and depth we can form not the slightest conception.

The Resurrection of her Son produced in Mary this prodigy: it absorbed her life, transformed it into the Risen Life of Jesus —a life wholly interior, invisible, separated from all created things and uninterruptedly united with God. Let us imitate our Mother in this. Let us remember that the more interior the life, the more perfect it is. A packed fire burns for a long time, but when it is opened up it soon goes out. There are few who really wish to live this life of annihilation, because it is the final immolation of self-love. But it is the lot of souls who, like Mary, desire to love only our Lord and to be known only to Him.

FATHER HERMANN'S VOCATION

In the life of Father Hermann, we are told that after his conversion this holy Religious heard Mary invite him to enter Carmel. He preserved for us the words she spoke as he thought he had heard them. They were very instructive.

"'Come to Carmel! There will I give thee a mysterious bread which makes one dream of Paradise: there will I give thee the wine which bringeth forth virgins; it is there that I sacrificed a Victim whose grateful odor sweetly ascends to the Throne of Jehovah. Come and eat the bread which I kneaded with the virginal milk of my virginal blood; come and drink the wine I drew forth from my most pure blood. If you wish to know, you must choose to follow; pay attention to the fruit, to the nourishment it offers; look at the fruit of my womb!'

"And at the same time Mary showed me the ostensorium. 'This is the fruit which is mine, and this fruit is the Eucharist.' Great God! the Eucharist," exclaimed Father Hermann. "Mary, you are the Mother of the Eucharist. You are giving me the Eucharist! You are daily feeding me with this Manna from heaven! You will bring my lips to touch the brim of this precious chalice overflowing with the Blood of my God! I will keep my heart to love Jesus in the Eucharist; to love Mary who gave Him to me." *(Life, by Sylvain, p. 381.)*

Practice—We should live, in union with Mary, the Risen Life that Jesus leads in the Most Blessed Sacrament.

Aspiration—Hail, Mary, Vessel of purest gold, which contains sweetness itself, Jesus Eucharistic, the Manna of our soul!

SIXTEENTH DAY

Mary, Our Mother in the Cenacle

I. It is to our best interest to honor with a particular devotion the life of Mary in the Cenacle, altogether given up to the service and glory of the Eucharist. We must try to catch something of her spirit and love, in order to render our Divine Savior present in our midst, a worship of adoration more pleasing and more perfect, in union with that which His most holy Mother offered Him. To become good servants of the Eucharist, we must be docile and devout children of Mary. It was not an empty claim over the heart of His Mother that Jesus gave us from the Cross. By that testament of love, we take His place in Mary's heart. That good Mother loves us henceforth as her true children.

Let us, then, breathe in Mary's spirit; it is the same as that of Jesus, for she received it from its Divine Source. She is full of His grace, in order to communicate it to us. She is the only true and perfect copy of His virtues; she labored for three and thirty years with the Divine Original constantly before her eyes. She knows all the secrets of the love of the Savior for mankind; she shares His unbounded love for us. Oh! with what tenderness and devotion does Mary love us! She loves us as only a Mother so good and so powerful can love.

II. Our Lady's mission is to form Jesus in us. This is the mission that He gave her on Calvary. When Mary would have died with Jesus at the foot of the Cross, when the flame of her virginal love was burning itself out before her Divine Son, our Lord seemed to say in confiding St John to her: "By My Sacrifice I became the Savior and the Father of the great human family; but these poor children must have a mother. Do thou be their Mother, O thou strong one. Love them even as thou hast loved Me, as I have loved them. It was through love for them that I became Man, through love for them that My Heavenly Father made thee My Mother. It is for them that I am giving My Blood and My life. I love them more than Myself, and I transfer to them all the claims that I have to thy maternal love. Whatever thou dost for them, will be done for Me. I confide to thee the fruits of My Redemption, the salvation of mankind, the care of My Church, the service of My Sacrament of Love. Form for Me true adorers in spirit and in truth, that they may adore Me as thou hast adored Me; that they may love Me as thou hast loved Me!"

This was Jesus' last legacy, signed with His Blood and ratified by the heart of Mary, His Blessed Mother.

She had ascended Calvary with Jesus, to die with Him; she came down therefrom with the beloved disciple, her adopted son, with the holy women, her daughters. Later, she would conduct them to the Eucharistic Cenacle, there to begin her Christian maternity at the foot of the Divine Sacrament.

It is she who will form a guard of honor for Jesus in the Eucharist; she it is who will train His servants. Oh! do not doubt it; if you have the happiness of knowing, loving and serving the Most Holy Sacrament, it is to Mary that you owe that happiness. It is she who asked the Heavenly Father to give you to her for the guard of love of the Eucharistic King. It is she who preserved you pure in the midst of the world, who led you by the hand to the foot of the Eucharistic Throne.

Oh! thank well this good Mother! You owe all the graces of your life to her, and the greatest of them all is that of loving and serving by the consecration of your entire life to Him, the King of kings on His Throne of Love.

SHE IS MY MOTHER

It is well known what tender love St Stanislaus Kostka had vowed to the Most Blessed Virgin.

SIXTEENTH DAY

When he was asked the reason for this lively affection he would reply, with a voice and look that betrayed his deep emotion: "She is my Mother!"

It happened that before he entered the Company of Jesus he became grievously ill; and as he was living with heretics he could not receive the Blessed Sacrament. For a heart so full of love for the Eucharist, this was a more cruel pain than the illness which was undermining his body. He had recourse to St Barbara, patroness of the dying, and his prayer was soon granted. The Saint appeared to him surrounded by angels who brought the Object of his desires: Holy Communion. But Mary herself was watching over this privileged child of her heart: she wished to manifest in a sensible form who it was that he had just received beneath the Sacramental veils. So she showed herself to him, holding her most dear Jesus in her arms; then she laid this inestimable Treasure on his bed. One cannot conceive the fervor, the respect, the tenderness and consolation which the saintly youth experienced in beholding his couch adorned with so precious a flower. From that moment he began to improve, and in a short time his illness disappeared and he was entirely cured, having been unable to resist the healing touch of the Author of life. *(Lives of the Saints, August 15.)*

Practice—Let us render to our Lady of the Most Blessed Sacrament, the reverence, the obedience and the love of a true child.

Aspiration—It is thou, O Mary most amiable, who dost nourish thy children with the Bread of immortality.

SEVENTEENTH DAY

Mary, Our Mistress in the Cenacle

I. "Disciple, behold thy Mother!" When Mary heard these words from the lips of her dying Son, words which mean so much to us, her soul suffered inexpressible anguish. What! the disciple instead of the Master; John instead of Jesus; the creature instead of the Son of God! But Our Blessed Mother lovingly accepts the substitution. She covered us with the Blood and the merits of her Divine Son, and began to love us with that boundless love which caused her to find happiness in tarrying here below for some twenty years, in order to nourish us with her love and her incomparable graces, in spite of her intense desire to be united immediately with her Son in glory.

Mary's mission will be to superintend our Christian education. Jesus acquired all the treasures of grace: Mary will have but to draw therefrom, to distribute the Bread that He left us, to make us follow the law that He gave us. Jesus could not remain among us in His glorified state, for we should have been afraid of Him. He remains, indeed, in the Blessed Sacrament, but His love deprives

Him of all exterior action, and chains Him there in order that He may be more appealing, more approachable.

But here is our Mother, who is also His; she possesses the secret of His Heart and of His life. She will accommodate the virtues of Jesus to our capacity, teach them to us in the appealing, homely fashion that a mother adopts with her child, so that we may more easily imitate them. If I dare say it, Mary will mold Jesus for us, make Him as gentle, as easy to approach and to imitate as is a mother by her little child.

O how beautiful, how touching will be the words of Jesus repeated by Mary's lips! How easy of imitation are His virtues—so heroic in themselves—when explained to us by Mary! How beautiful Jesus will appear to us when painted by Mary! How easy our education will be under such a Mistress!

II. She will conceive, will form and perfect Jesus in us—and she will give us to Him. The Father has delivered His Son to her, that she may give Him to us. Mankind was unworthy to receive the Word direct from God, so Mary was our Mediatrix in the Incarnation, and she continues to exercise that function. No one comes to the knowledge of Jesus·Christ and embraces His holy law, but through her; no one obtains the saving gift of faith, but by Mary's prayers. Her mission, to which she is ever faithful,

is to give us Jesus. He must be received
from her hands, and in vain we seek Him
elsewhere. Moreover, Jesus will increase in
us only by Mary; all the graces which fos-
ter our spiritual life will come to us only
through her. It was under her maternal direction that He grew at Nazareth, and He
wishes us to follow the same law. We see
in the Gospels, also, that all His principal
favors were granted through Mary and with
her. By her He sanctified St John the Baptist; He glorified His Father and constituted
Himself our Model at Nazareth under her
eyes; He strengthened the faith of His disciples at Cana by performing His first miracle at her request; lastly, on the Cross, He
solemnly charged her with the duty of forming us. It is, in a word, by Mary that He
will perfect Himself in us. The perfection
of Jesus in us is, properly speaking, the
work of the Holy Spirit; but as the Spirit
of Love willed to make His Masterpiece, the
Sacred Humanity of Jesus, in union with
Mary, so also to establish in us the perfect
image of the Savior, to transform us into
"other Christs," He claims Mary's coöpera-
tion. The more resemblance to Mary He
finds in the soul, the more powerfully He
works therein. Ask any of those saintly
souls in whom the love of Jesus reigns supreme from whence they got this love, and
they will tell you it was from Mary. Does

she not possess the secret of the Spirit of Jesus in all its plenitude? She reflects Jesus as the Word shows forth the Father. It is for her to give us the family spirit, as it were. To accomplish this she takes into her maternal heart all the qualities, all the virtues of Jesus, and then presents them to us in such a way as to encourage us to imitate them. Through Mary's love we progress to the sanctity of Jesus; in living by Mary's holiness, we live in Jesus' holiness.

III. How beautiful it would be to study Mary instilling into the mind and heart of the child its first knowledge of Jesus; then, as a youth, arousing him to generosity of service for Jesus; preparing him for First Holy Communion; leading him to the choice of a holy and suitable state of life! This education of the young man by Mary will have a permanent influence on his life; conducted in so gently a manner, made so enchanting through her love and piety, it leaves an impression that not even dissipation can efface, a habit of reverence, of love for her, that remains, sometimes, even when God is forgotten. Mary's sublime and gentle image accompanies him through life. Happy is he who has received from her his first lessons in holiness; Mary will ever be to him a lever to raise him from sin; her name will always arouse in his heart a thrill of love.

Mary it is, also, who educates the Christian maiden. From infancy, she inspires her with piety, with love for Jesus. She enkindles in her heart a noble flame of divine ambition. She shows her her own immaculate lily of virginity, which constitutes her crown, then pressing her to her bosom with a chaste and maternal embrace, she says to her: "O my daughter, be a lily, be the spouse of my Divine Son! Give Him thy heart and receive His virginal ring. Look at my crown, the reward of my love for virginity, and be my daughter in a twofold manner!"

Thus it is that Mary forms, guards, and defends virgins. *"Adducentur virgines post eam."* Mary is their Queen.

Such is the education given by Mary; she makes piety sweet and easy. What she did in the first days of the Church, she does still. Like us, the Apostles had the Eucharist. But the first education in the home is not given by the father; an education which is destitute of maternal tenderness always shows the signs. Sanctity that is fashioned by Jesus alone has an austere character; that which Jesus and Mary form together is more attractive—witness St John and St Paul. Let Mary, then, lead us to Jesus; let her teach us to know and to love Him as she knows and loves Him. In this alone consists true sanctity and perfect happiness.

MARY LOVES JESUS IN US

It is when we possess our Lord in our heart that Mary surrounds us with her most maternal affection, because then she sees her Beloved Son in us.

The Abbess, St Opportune, being at the point of death, asked for the Sacred Body of our Lord, and such was her devotion in receiving Him, that Jesus not only showed her the greatest marks of love, but she saw Mary also descend near her bed to console and sustain her in her last struggle. The good Abbess earnestly entreated her to watch over her daughters, and the interests of the monastery. She then stretched her arms towards Mary as though to embrace her, and commended her soul with its last sigh into her hands. (Nicolao Laghi, *trat.* II, *c.* xlvii.)

Practice—We should pray to Mary that all those in their last agony may receive Holy Viaticum worthily.

Aspiration—Hail, Mary, celestial Cloud which sheds the Eucharist over the world, like a beneficent dew!

EIGHTEENTH DAY

Our Lady of the Cenacle

Let us follow our Mother to the Cenacle and listen to the lessons that she there teaches us, lessons that she has received from her Divine Son, with whom she conversed day and night. She is the faithful echo of His Heart and of His love. Let us love Mary tenderly; let us labor under her maternal eye, and pray by her side. Let us be her truly devoted children, for by so doing, we shall honor Jesus who has given her to us for our Mother, that she may teach us how to love Him by the example of her own life.

Place yourself, then, under Mary's direction; think her thoughts, speak her words of love, imitate her manners, perform her actions, share her sufferings, and all in her will speak to you of Jesus, of His highest service, of God's greatest glory.

Honor in Mary, at the foot of the Tabernacle, all the mysteries of her life, for all these were stations, as it were, leading to the Cenacle. In Mary's life there you will find the model and the consolation of your own life. In the Cenacle, this august Queen kneels as adoratrix and servant of the Most Blessed Sacrament: kneel at your Mother's side and pray with her, and in so doing, you will continue her Eucharistic life on earth.

When you receive Holy Communion, clothe yourself with the virtues and merits of Mary, your mother, and you will thus communicate with her faith and with her devotion. O how happy Jesus will be to find in you the image of His lovable and holy Mother!

When you labor to promote the Eucharistic reign of our Lord, unite yourself with Mary's intention and with her joy when she worked for Jesus in the Blessed Sacrament, and you will be happy!

Oh, how Mary will love you if you serve her Jesus well! How she will protect you if you labor only for the glory of Jesus! How she will enrich you if you live only for the love of Jesus! You will render her still more Mother, since you enable her to discharge more perfectly her mission as Mother of the adorers of her Son Jesus.

But you must be modest as she was. Remember her modesty in the Angel's presence, and reflect on the modesty with which she served her Son in the Blessed Sacrament.

Be pure as Mary. Remember that in order to preserve the flower of her virginity she was ready to sacrifice even the glory of the Divine Maternity.

Be humble as Mary—entirely lost in her own nothingness, entirely abandoned to God's grace.

Be sweet and amiable as Mary. She was the embodiment of the sweetness of the Heart of Jesus.

Be devoted as Mary. Mary loved to the extent of Calvary—she loved even unto death. It was on Calvary that she became the Mother of love. There only will you become a true adorer, worthy of the Cenacle, worthy of Jesus and Mary.

THE IMAGE AND THE REALITY

There is no doubt that the respect we show the pictures of our Lord and the care we take in adorning them must be very pleasing to Mary, and this devotion has often been rewarded by extraordinary manifestations. Nevertheless, because we look upon the figures, they should not make us forget the adorable reality which shows itself to a loving heart alone.

The venerable servant of God, Theresa Mexia, of the Order of St Dominic, had great devotion to a statue of the Infant Jesus carried in His Mother's arms: she adorned it with flowers; she clothed it in rare materials, and lavished upon it every attention her tender love suggested. Now, this is the wonderful lesson that the Blessed Virgin taught her. One day when she presented the Infant Jesus with a very carefully embroidered dress, she said to Him: "Come, my Beloved. Receive this dress offered by your unworthy servant." The Child left His Mother's arms and came down upon the altar that her wish might be granted.

She dressed the image in its beautiful gown, all the while paying no attention to the altar and the Tabernacle where our Lord dwelt in Person. But a voice was heard, saying: "Theresa, thou art quite taken up with this image. How is it that thou dost forget the living reality?" The saintly girl understood the lesson, and without ceasing to adorn her dear statue of the Infant God, she devoted her attention towards adorning the altar and the Eucharistic Tabernacle: with great effort she even succeeded in collecting enough gold and silver to have constructed one of the richest and most beautiful Tabernacles to be found in Spain.

Practice—Let us labor zealously for the adornment of the Eucharistic altars, particularly for those of poor churches.

Aspiration—The Lord, O Mary, has adorned thee as the Tabernacle of His choice, and Jesus Hostia has made it His delight to dwell in thee!

NINETEENTH DAY

LIFE OF ADORATION IN UNION WITH MARY

I. In considering attentively the reasons that induced our Lord to leave us His Blessed Mother and so separate Himself from her, it seems to me that He did so because He was distrustful of our weakness and inconstancy. Our Lord feared that men, not knowing how to find and adore Him in His Sacrament, would become discouraged and would forget Him. The child, as we know, does not search long for something he wants; if he does not find it at once, he gives up and seeks something else. This is what our Lord feared for us; so He left us His Mother, whose mission it should be to take us by the hand and lead us to His Tabernacle. The Blessed Virgin, then, became our Mother, in view of the Eucharist. To her is entrusted the task of showing us how to find our Bread of Life, of making us appreciate and desire that Heavenly Food; it is her mission to form us for adoration. After our Lord's Ascension, she gathered about her a community of pious women at Jerusalem; she dwelt with them, sharing with them her treasure of grace and love. Her influence extended to the disciples and to the first Christians. Like a true Mother, she trained her children to be faithful to the duties of their state and to practice virtue. What Mary did then, she will do for us now. She will instruct us, show us our Lord in the Eucharist, causing us to take part in her pious devotion to His service—for all that a Mother possesses belongs to her children. Mary being our Mother, then, will educate us. When the child lets its attention wander from its work, the mother is there to recall it to its duty; if it is sick, she cares for it. She does not leave the child to itself, she fulfills her duty as educator. Mary, in the same way, will train you; she will instill into you her method of adoration; she will even make your adoration in and for you, for only she can inspire you with the spirit of true and fervent adoration. It is only a mother's heart that can make itself perfectly understood by her child. The Blessed Virgin will say to you: "Come, adore with me." Our Lord has given us Mary to be the bond of union between Him and us. Mary gives us the first attraction to Jesus. The child instinctively goes first to its mother, then the mother leads it to its father; it does not go to him of its own accord, its instinct is to follow its mother. Our Lord, then, has given us Mary for our Mother, to be an easy center of attraction. Before we knew the Eucharist, we knew the name of our Mother —we already loved her. Mary attracted us to herself: she trained us to the virtues necessary for the Eucharistic life. It was fitting that it should be thus, and it is evident to me that there will be no true vocations to the Blessed Sacrament, no real devotion to the Eucharist, except those that have been formed by Mary. No, the infant can only be reared in its mother's arms, and on her breast. To be pleasing to the Heart of our Lord, all vocations must pass through Mary's hands.

II. Reflect for a moment on your past life. Had you not a great devotion to the Blessed Virgin before devoting yourself to the Eucharist? You longed to possess her purity, her love. Without knowing Mary's Eucharistic life, you said: "Oh, if I only had her virtues with which to serve Jesus!" That was the first attraction for you. You behaved like the little child, who when it cannot take its mother's hands, grasps her apron, or the hem of her dress; if it leaves her but for an instant it thinks itself lost. The mother is the center—she is always the center—we need to dwell always with her, for we need her at all times.

The Blessed Virgin is not like the Saints, who obtain for us certain specific graces, and that but occasionally. She obtains for us every grace; we have always need of her. Again, it is the mother who teaches the child the little compliment which she herself has prepared for the father; she knows the father's tastes so well. Do you see the analogy? I would say to each one of you: adore our Lord in the company of His Blessed Mother. I do not say abide in Mary. No. Jesus is there before you in order that you may speak to Him direct; but do so *with* Mary; live in her company. Since our Lord has given her to you as directress, never make your adoration without her.

Say to her: "Sweet Mother, come with me, for a mother always accompanies her child, and without thee I shall not know what to say!"

Picture to yourself Mary on her knees in the Cenacle; see her adoring her Son hidden in the Eucharist. Oh, how pleasing to Him were her words! How well she knew how to touch her Son's Heart. Kneel there at Mary's side; stay with her. Let your adoration and homage be one with hers. Say: "O Jesus, I do not know how to adore, but I offer Thee the words, the ecstasies of Thy Mother's heart, which is mine also. I do not know how to adore, but I repeat to Thee her adoration: for sinners; for the conversion of the world; and for all the needs of the Church!" By so doing, you will rejoice Mary's heart. She will show you to Jesus, saying: "Behold, my Son, how I live anew in this soul, how I again adore Thee in him and by him!"

Oh! if any one should honor, love and serve Mary, it is he whose profession it is to live for the Eucharist. He has need of Mary in order to adore rightly; he must be one with her in adoration.

Ah! let the Blessed Virgin, then, govern your life; let her lead you to Jesus! She desires but one thing—the glory of her Divine Son and your happiness!

THE FOUNDATION OF THE CITY OF MONTREAL

It is impossible to read of the beginnings of the City of Montreal, in Canada, without being deeply moved.

On the 18th of May 1642, M. de Maisonneuve and his intrepid companions landed on the island where later on the city was to be built. Lifting their voices in psalms and hymns in the excess of their gratitude, their first care before undertaking anything else was to have the Divine Sacrifice solemnly celebrated, and the Sacred Host remained exposed all that day, which was entirely devoted to pious exercises and thanksgiving to the Adorable Person of the Savior present in the Sacred Species, and who thus took possession of the territory.

But by whom was this demonstration prepared? Was it not Mary who, six years before on the Feast of the Purification, had inspired M. Olivier and M. de la Danversière simultaneously with the idea of sending some priests and religious to evangelize Canada? Yes, it was certainly the Mother of God who impelled the first explorers to sail towards Montreal, so that they might there erect a throne for her Son. But, as ever, Jesus will not be outdone in generosity. The city which was soon to rise on the banks of the St Lawrence River will be called preëminently Ville Marie (Maryville), the City of Mary, and its Bishop will justly bear the title of "Vicar of Mary." Mary had erected a throne for Jesus at Montreal; Jesus wanted His Mother to have a throne beside His own. Oh! how the thrones of our Lady of the Most Blessed Sacrament are multiplying throughout the entire world. (From Lépicier, *The Most Holy Virgin in Relation to the Most Blessed Sacrament.*)

Practice—As much as possible prepare yourself for Holy Communion by assisting at Holy Mass.

Aspiration—The Divine Sparrow of the Tabernacle has found in thee His nest, O Blessed Virgin, and He lovingly dwells therein.

TWENTIETH DAY

Mary's Adoration of Faith and Respect

I. How much might be said of Mary's life of adoration in the Cenacle! Twenty years passed in that holy place in which Jesus instituted the Eucharist, in which He set up His first Tabernacle! Mary was wholly employed in adoring and honoring Him in His Eucharistic life. She passed the greater part of her days and nights at the foot of that divine Tabernacle, for there was Jesus, her Son and her God.

Mary's adoration began as soon as she set out from her poor little cell on her way to the Cenacle. She walked with downcast eyes, grave and modest step, in perfect recollection, preparing herself thus to appear before the God of the Eucharist.

As soon as she came before the Tabernacle, she prostrated herself with profound respect and devotion, then composed her senses in a simple act of recollection. She kept her body erect, her hands joined or crossed on her breast or, when alone, frequently raised in supplication towards the Tabernacle, on which her eyes were constantly fixed.

TWENTIETH DAY

II. Mary adored with most submissive faith. She adored her hidden Son, veiled under a strange form. But her love found its way through the veil, even to the very Feet of Jesus, which she venerated with the most tender respect; then to His holy, venerable Hands, which had consecrated and distributed the Bread of Life; she blessed the Sacred Mouth which had pronounced the adorable words: "This is My Body! . . . This is My Blood!" She adored that Heart so inflamed with love, whence had issued the Holy Eucharist. Mary would have wished to annihilate herself completely before the Divine Majesty annihilated in the Sacrament, that by so doing she might render Him due homage and love.

III. Mary's adoration was profound, interior, and intimate. It was the gift of herself. She offered herself wholly to the service of loving God in the Eucharist; for love knows no reservation, lays down no conditions; it thinks no more of self, lives no longer for self; it is as a stranger to itself, it lives only for the God whom it loves. All in Mary turned toward the Blessed Sacrament as toward its center and end. A current of grace and love was established between the Adorable Heart of Jesus Hostia and the adoring heart of Mary; they were two flames that burned as one. God was perfectly adored by His creature!

IV. With the example of Mary before him, let the adorer kneel before the Blessed Sacrament with the most profound respect; let him, like Mary, recollect himself, and, in spirit, take his place at her side while he adores. Let him come before our Lord with that modesty, that interior and exterior recollection, which so fittingly prepares the soul for the angelic office of adoration.

Under the Eucharistic veils that hide the Sacred Humanity, let us adore Jesus with Mary's faith and with that of Holy Church —those two Mothers that the Savior has, in His love, given us. Let us adore our God as though we saw Him, heard Him; for an earnest faith sees, hears and touches with more certitude than the senses themselves.

MARY PROCURES AND ACCOMPANIES THE HOLY VIATICUM

A pious girl deprived of this world's goods, rich in her faith alone, and very devoted to Mary, was, to her great regret, at the point of death without receiving the Body of her beloved Savior. The Mother of Goodness came to her aid. Surrounded by angels she appeared to Blessed Oderic of Port-Mahon, who was crossing a forest alone. "There is," she told him, "a faithful servant of mine near-by who is dying, and who ardently desires to receive the Holy Viaticum. Her parish priest is absent; I want you to take his place. I will myself guide you to the church and then to the sick one, as I wish to be present at her last Communion."

TWENTIETH DAY

The Blessed one obeyed, and taking the Blessed Sacrament carried It devoutly, Mary accompanied him, her face radiant with gentle majesty. Who shall tell what homage of respect and love she rendered to her Son hidden beneath the Sacramental Species!

The sick girl received the Sacred Body of Jesus in the presence of the Blessed Virgin. I leave you to imagine what consolation flooded her soul, and if she was not well rewarded for having asked this good Mother for her most dear Jesus, whom she never refuses to those who turn to her. (Rossignoli.)

Practice—Let us, in union with Mary, accompany the Blessed Sacrament when It is taken to the sick.

Aspiration—O Queen of Goodness, we contemplate thee at the side of Jesus Eucharistic, the King of kings!

TWENTY-FIRST DAY

Mary's Adoration of Thanksgiving

I. To her act of humble faith, to her adoration of deep self-annihilation, Mary added thanksgiving. After remaining lost in the thought of all the dignity and the divine majesty that are veiled in the Sacrament, she would look up at this Thabor of Love in order to contemplate Its beauty and enjoy Its ineffable goodness. Mary gave thanks to Jesus for His love in the gift of the Eucharist, that sovereign act of His infinite bounty. Her thanksgiving was perfect, because she understood the greatness of this Gift.

Oh, how happy Mary was when before the Last Supper Jesus revealed to her that the hour for the triumph of His love had come, that He was about to institute His Adorable Sacrament, by which each of the Faithful could share her happiness and, like her, receive Him into his breast, see Him, after a fashion, and in His Sacramental state enjoy all the graces and experience the mysteries of His mortal life: "After this Gift, in which I exhaust My power, I have nothing more to give to man, except heaven!"

At this glorious news, Mary prostrated herself at the feet of Jesus, poured out her soul in an effusion of loving gratitude for this marvel of love which He was to accomplish for His unworthy creatures. She offered herself to serve Him in His Adorable Sacrament; she consented to delay the hour of her reward, in order that she might remain an adorer on earth, commissioned to guard, to serve the Eucharist, happy to die at the foot of the divine Tabernacle.

II. In her adoration in the Cenacle, Mary daily renewed her thanksgiving: "How good Thou art, O my Savior!" she exclaimed. "How good Thou art, my Savior and my Son! How couldst Thou love man to such a degree as to give him more than he can receive, love him more than he can appreciate, invent what his heart can never understand! For love of him Thou dost exhaust Thy power and the treasures of Thy Heart!"

Then Mary gave thanks to each of the powers of Jesus' soul, to each of the Savior's members which had coöperated in the institution of the Eucharist, offering to them the flames of love that consumed her heart.

Oh! with what satisfaction, with what happiness, must Jesus have received this first homage of His Blessed Mother, the first that was rendered to His Sacrament! Oh! how His Heart must have rejoiced at having left Mary His Sacramental Presence for her consolation! For Jesus would have instituted the Eucharist for Mary alone. We need not be astonished at this, for Mary's adoration and thanksgiving were of more value in the eyes of Jesus than the united homage of all the Saints.

Mary's thanksgiving was, furthermore, most agreeable to Jesus because the recognition of benefits received and gratitude for them please Him above all else. That is all He expects from us. To adore by thanksgiving is to adore well. It is to recognize the first of His attributes, the one which above all others He came to earth to manifest—His goodness. Let us dwell on it at length when we are at His feet.

Let us, then, return thanks through Mary. A child receives a gift, but it is his mother who thanks the donor for him. So our thanksgiving, united with that of Mary, will be perfect and most acceptable to the Heart of Jesus.

A CHILD'S PRESERVATION FROM FIRE

In the early ages of the Church it was the custom to give the little children, who still preserved their baptismal innocence, the Consecrated Particles remaining after the Communion of the Faithful.

One day the young son of a Jewish glass-blower from Constantinople, who was going to school with the Christian children, was taken to the church with them, and innocently presented himself with the others to receive the Fragments of the Holy Eucharist.

On his return home he told his father what he had just done. The father being a brutal man and belonging to the class of Jews filled with animosity towards the Christian religion, became violently enraged. He seized the unfortunate child and cast him alive into a burning furnace. Shortly after, the mother, who had been absent, returned to her home, and not knowing what had occurred, asked everywhere what had become of her son. As no one could give her any news of him, she ran about the various quarters of the town looking for him, but all her steps were useless. Three days passed. Sad and inconsolable and bemoaning the loss of her son, she began to call him by name as though he were there.

All of a sudden, O wonder! she hears a voice giving her the tender name of mother. Much disturbed, she runs to the furnace whence the voice seemed to issue. At first she cannot believe that her child can be in the midst of those devouring flames; but the call is repeated more distinctly this time; she can doubt no longer. She opens the door and looks. Strange spectacle! She sees her child in this burning furnace, but still full of life.

She calls her neighbors to the rescue; every one rushes in to witness the prodigy.

The child is taken out from the burning furnace. He is questioned and asked how he managed to fall into it and remain alive in such devouring flames. He tells them that it was his father who cast him into it, for having assisted at Christian ceremonies; but that a tall lady, dazzling with light, had preserved him from the flames by covering him with her mantle, and had even given him food to appease his hunger; that this lady looked exactly like the picture of the Blessed Virgin he had seen in the Christian church.

Every one then understood that it was the Virgin Mary who had saved and preserved his life by protecting him from the flames. The Emperor, having been told how this unnatural father had behaved, had him arrested and condemned to the torture. Instead of being converted, the wretch stubbornly persisted in his error. As to the mother and child, they asked to be instructed in the Catholic religion, and receiving Baptism became fervent Christians.

Practice—Let us pray incessantly for seminarians, the altar boys of our different parishes, and for all who work around the altar, that they may acquit themselves with piety and reverence of their holy functions.

Aspiration—O Mary! perfect handmaid of our Jesus Eucharistic, we bless thee!

TWENTY-SECOND DAY

Mary's Eucharistic Contemplation

I. Contemplation naturally follows adoration and thanksgiving, while, at the same time, it nourishes and perfects them. Eucharistic contemplation is the study of Jesus in the Blessed Sacrament, in which the soul considers in detail His marvelous goodness in instituting this Sacrament, studies its motives, examines its sacrifices, weighs its Gift, and appreciates its love.

The first fruit of Eucharistic contemplation is the recollection of the soul in our Lord, in which it discovers the mystery of His perfections and the love of this ineffable Gift of the Eucharist. This consideration of the excessive love of Jesus in preparing, instituting and perpetuating the Blessed Sacrament, produces in us first adoration, then praise, and lastly an expansion of love. The soul goes out of self in order to unite with Jesus, in order to adhere to the Divine Object of its contemplation. Hence it follows that contemplation is the essential part of adoration.

II. Mary's contemplation before the Eucharist was of a nature that no words are adequate to describe. Jesus Christ alone, who was its Object, knew its value. Mary had the most complete knowledge of the love that Jesus had shown in instituting the Eucharist. She knew what combats His Heart had to sustain, the sacrifices exacted of Him by the institution of this Sacrament: combats of His love against the incredulity and the indifference of the greater part of mankind; combats of His sanctity against impiety, the blasphemy and the sacrileges of which His Sacrament would be the Object, not only on the part of heretics, but even on the part of His friends; combats of His goodness against the ingratitude of Christians who neglect to receive Him in Holy Communion, refusing thereby His richest graces, His most tender invitation. But the love of Jesus triumphed over all these obstacles: "I shall love men in spite of everything; and their malice can neither discourage nor conquer My goodness!"

Mary had followed these combats, she had shared these sacrifices whose triumph she now witnesses; and she lives them over again in her adoration. She recalls them to the Savior, and she exalts the love that had made Him a victor.

III. In order to appreciate the gift of the Eucharist at Its just value, the adorer ought to go as Mary did, and with her, to Its source, to the sacrifices It demanded of our

Lord's love. If that love is beautiful on Calvary, it is even more beautiful in the Cenacle and on the Altar, for there it is love forever immolated. The contemplation of those combats and of that victory will suggest to the adorer what he owes in return to a God so good. Then, with Mary, His Divine Mother, he will offer himself to Jesus Eucharistic with his whole heart, to bless Him, to thank Him for so much love. He will devote himself to honoring the various states of our Sacramental Jesus, practicing in his life those virtues that the Savior continues and glorifies so admirably therein. He will honor the profound humility of the Savior which goes so far as to annihilate Himself entirely under the Sacred Species. He will honor the abnegation of His power and glory which makes Him the Prisoner of men. He will honor His obedience, which makes Him the servant of all. He will take Mary as the pattern of his Eucharistic life in order to aid him in his practical study. He will love her and confide himself to her as to the Mother of Adorers, which is the title dearest to her heart and most glorious to Jesus.

THE TENDER PROTECTION OF MARY

Several years ago, during one of the internal wars that periodically break out in China, bands of insurgents marched on the little Christian village of Ton-nien-fang, in the northern part of the Cheusi, and began by encircling it.

The poor earthen wall protecting the village and the few guns in the hands of the Christians, evidently did not constitute sufficient elements of defense against the hordes of savage aggressors.

The situation was very serious, and the Apostolic Vicar judged it prudent to have the Sacred Species consumed, in order to avoid certain profanation. Yielding, however, to the earnest entreaties and supplications of the Franciscan Missionary Nuns of Mary, who were in the village, instead of consuming the Sacred Species, he organized at the orphan asylum a solemn nocturnal adoration before the Most Blessed Sacrament exposed.

The faith and fervor of prayer manifested in this supreme devotion can easily be understood.

As the day dawned, the Christians found, to their great astonishment that the enemies had raised the siege and were departing.

Later, on being questioned as to the motive of this sudden change, the soldiers related that they had been halted before the village walls by the sudden appearance of a "White Lady" who held in her hands something resplendent as the sun. The small band of Christians was saved! (From Serafiche, *Missione delle Franciscane Missionarie di Maria*—1928.)

Practice—Let us pray incessantly to Mary for the interests of the Eucharist.

Aspiration—O Mary, no one can approach so near to Jesus as thou!

TWENTY-THIRD DAY

Mary's Adoration of Propitiation

I. Mary adored her very dear Son in His character of Victim immolated perpetually on our Altars, incessantly imploring grace and mercy for sinners, through the merits of His death. Mary adored the Savior on this new Calvary upon which His love crucified Him. She offered Him to God for the salvation of her new family, and the sight of Jesus on the Cross with His gaping wounds, renewed in her soul the martyrdom of her compassion. At Holy Mass, she again beheld her crucified Jesus shedding His Blood abundantly, in the midst of suffering and opprobrium, abandoned by men, abandoned even by God—dying in the supreme act of His love. Mary adoring her God present on the altar by the Consecration, shed abundant tears: at the sight of those who make no account of this august Sacrifice, and so render fruitless this Mystery of their Redemption; at the sight of those who dare to sin against, to despise this Adorable Victim offered under their very eyes for their salvation.

Mary would willingly have offered a thousand deaths to repair so many outrages; for these unfortunate creatures who are incurring this guilt are her own children, the children whom Jesus had confided to her when dying. Poor Mother! Is not one Calvary sufficient for her? Why renew her sorrows daily and pierce her heart anew with words of impiety?

However, Mary, as the best of Mothers, instead of rejecting and cursing these sinners, took upon herself the penalty of their crimes; she expiated them by suffering; she herself became a victim at the foot of the altar, imploring grace and mercy for her guilty children.

II. Mary adored Jesus in the state of Prisoner which Jesus assumed by uniting Himself inseparably to the Sacred Species. She contemplated His glorified Body, His feet, His hands condemned to material immobility; His tongue speechless, His Soul without exterior expansion, His love without power, without wings—fettered, unable to show man aught but His chains of love.

"O happy bonds that keep Jesus in our midst," said Mary, "be ye blessed! Ye are fiery chains that attach me to this divine Tabernacle! Silence of my God, how eloquent art thou to my heart! Sacred members of my Savior, you are still dearer to me than when the nails fastened you to the Cross, or when the folds of the winding-sheet encompassed you! It is love that keeps you here, and forever, in order that I may make of Jesus my Treasure, my Prisoner of love, the Companion of my captivity here below, the God of my heart!"

III. Mary adored the hidden state of Jesus' Divinity and Humanity in His Sacrament, veiled that man might not attach himself to the glory and beauty of His Person, but should go freely to the Divinity of the Word. Jesus thus veiled Himself only to spiritualize man's faith, to purify his heart, to stimulate his love, and to attract him to the Infinite, to an ever new and ever increasing beauty.

Mary, then, adored Jesus veiled in His Sacrament, but visible to her love. She saw behind the cloud the beauty of this Sun, who manifests His ardor by the light He gives to our soul, who manifests His presence by His sweetness.

Mary honored the hidden life of Jesus by a retired and solitary life. She passed the greater part of her time in making reparation for ungrateful man. At sight of the Eucharistic annihilation of Jesus, she wished to be annihilated also, changed into a sacramental species, without life of her own. She had, in fact, transformed her natural life into that of Jesus, as the bread is transformed into the substance of Jesus Christ.

And so at the sight of His Divine Mother at His feet, the Savior consoled Himself for man's desertion. He loved the sacrifices that He had so generously made, and He preferred His state of annihilation to that of His glory. Mary, His Mother and the Mother of all adorers, made amends to Him for everything, and the love of Jesus found inexpressible satisfaction in receiving her prayers and her tears shed for the salvation of the world.

MARY'S INSTRUCTION ON THE MISFORTUNE OF MAKING BAD COMMUNIONS

We are going to relate below some of the words addressed by the Blessed Virgin to Mother Mary of Jesus on Communion. This is what she one day revealed to her: "If Godly love for the neighbor had such power within me, judge, my daughter, what must have been the vehemence of the love I felt for our Lord Himself when I received Him at the altar! I will here reveal to you a secret in regard to what happened to me when I received Him for the first time from St Peter's hands. It is this: the Most High allowed my love to act so violently within me that my heart really opened as I desired it should, and allowed my consecrated Son to enter and dwell therein, as a King upon His throne. You will understand by this, my very dear daughter, that could I be subject to any kind of sorrow in the glory which I enjoy, that which would cause me very great pain would be to see the frightful temerity of men who dare to receive the Sacred Body of my Most Holy Son—some soiled by horrible crimes, others without devotion, without respect, and nearly all of them without considering the importance, without weighing the value of that Host, which is nothing less than God Himself, the germ of eternal life or of eternal death. Fear, then, this danger, my daughter; weep over it for so many children of the Church; ask our Lord for their salvation, and profit by my teaching by endeavoring to become worthy to penetrate more deeply into this mystery of love.

"And when you partake of It, banish all thoughts of earthly things from your understanding; remember only that you are going to receive God Himself; make every effort to show Him your love, your humility, and your gratitude. And, even so, you may be very sure that you will always remain far below what this venerable Mystery deserves." *(Cité Mystique, p.* III, I. VII, *c.* vii.)

Practice—Let us assist at Mass frequently in order to repair, in union with Mary, the crime of those who fail to fulfill this command of the Church.

Aspiration—O Mary, thou art the true mystical Table whereon we find the delicious Food of our soul, Jesus Eucharistic!

TWENTY-FOURTH DAY

Mary's Prayer of Adoration

I. Mary devoted herself exclusively to the Eucharistic glory of Jesus. She knew that it was the desire of the Eternal Father to make the Eucharist known, loved and served by all men; that the need of Jesus' Heart was to communicate to all men His gifts of grace and glory. She knew, too, that it was the mission of the Holy Spirit to extend and perfect in the hearts of men the reign of Jesus Christ, and that the Church had been founded only to give Jesus to the world. All Mary's desire, then, was to make Him known in His Sacrament. Her intense love for Jesus felt the need of expanding in this way, of consecrating itself—as a kind of relief, as it were—because of her own inability to glorify Him as much as she desired.

Ever since Calvary, all men were her children. She loved them with a Mother's tenderness and longed for their supreme good as for her own; therefore, she was consumed with the desire to make Jesus in the Blessed Sacrament known to all, to inflame all hearts

TWENTY-FOURTH DAY 133

with His love, to see them enchained to His loving service.

To obtain this favor, Mary passed her time at the foot of the Most Adorable Sacrament, in prayer and penance. There she treated of the world's salvation. In her boundless zeal, she embraced the needs of the Faithful everywhere, for all time to come, who would inherit the Holy Eucharist and be Its adorers.

But the mission dearest to Mary's heart was that of constant prayer for the success of the preaching and the missionary labors of the Apostles and of all the members of Jesus Christ's priesthood. It is not surprising, then, that those Apostolic workers so easily converted entire kingdoms, for Mary remained constantly at the foot of the Throne of Mercy, supplicating on their behalf the Savior's benevolence. Her prayers converted countless souls, and as every conversion is the fruit of prayer, and since Mary's prayer could meet no refusal, the Apostles had in this Mother of Mercy their most powerful helper. "Blessed is he for whom Mary prays!"

II. Eucharistic adorers share Mary's life and mission of prayer at the foot of the Most Blessed Sacrament. It is the most beautiful of all missions, and it holds no perils. It is the most holy, for in it all the virtues are practiced. It is, moreover, the most necessary to the Church, which has even more need of prayerful souls than of powerful preachers; of men of penance rather than of men of eloquence. To-day more than ever have we need of men who, by their self-immolation, disarm the anger of God inflamed by the ever-increasing crimes of nations. We must have souls who by their importunity re-open the treasures of grace which the indifference of the multitude has closed. We must have true adorers; that is to say, men of fervor and of sacrifice. When there are many such souls around their Divine Chief, God will be glorified, Jesus will be loved, and society will once more become Christian, conquered for Jesus Christ by the apostolate of Eucharistic prayer.

III. Mary's apostolate, moreover, consisted in the very persuasive preaching of example. Such sermons suit one and all, and a soul zealous to make the Eucharist known and loved will, in union with Mary, devote itself thereto with the greatest earnestness. With what modesty and reverence will not the perfect adorer conduct himself before the Blessed Sacrament! He will conduct himself as do the Angels before the Throne of God. Entirely penetrated by faith and absorbed in the Divine Presence, he pays no attention to any one or to anything around him.

And he will never present himself before our Lord without being suitably and modestly clothed, as if for a ceremonious visit. Any negligence in dress, or carelessness of manner on his part would indicate little faith and a disorderly interior.

Mary remained kneeling at the feet of her God as long as she was able to do so. This is the posture adopted by Holy Church as most suited to adoration—the homage of the body, the humility of faith. Kneeling at the feet of Jesus is love's favorite position.

Respect in the holy place, above all before the Most Holy Sacrament, ought to be the characteristic exterior virtue of adorers. This respect is the solemn profession of their faith, and, at the same time, it is the grace of their piety and fervor; for God always punishes irreverence in His sanctuary by a weakening of faith and by the withdrawal of the grace of devotion. He who is irreverent or indecorous before our Lord should not be astonished at the coldness that he experiences in prayer. This is but a small part of the punishment he merits, he deserves to be expelled from God's presence as a rude, unmannerly fellow, or a senseless fool.

Let us, then, be very exacting in showing respect. Let us maintain a reserved exterior and a devout attitude; let us observe a rigorous silence and an absolute guard over the senses. When in church, we should see only Jesus Christ; friends and acquaintances should then be ignored. Jesus is our all. The courtier has his eyes only on the king, honors the king alone. At sight of the profound, religious respect of adorers, worldlings should be forced to say: "There is something *real* here!" The weak, the tepid will blush for their lukewarmness, and once more recognize Jesus Christ—for example is the royal lesson of wisdom and a most fruitful apostolate.

OUR LADY OF FIRST COMMUNION

Forming children for this great act in life, preparing their hearts for this first visit from Jesus —oh, without doubt this is the sweetest mission of Mary's tenderness.

There was once a mother who one day had a sweet vision. The Virgin Mary stood beside the cradle of her child; she smiled upon him and covered his little couch with flowers.... When Alexander Bertius could speak, his first words were: Jesus and Mary. He grew up under the shadow of the crucifix. By the light received in his Baptism he already had a glimpse in the depths of his own heart of tiny particles, seeming impurities whence the bad grain might spring. This child of five remembered Mary's promises and caresses: armed with a discipline, he chastised his delicate members for the instincts towards evil which he felt in himself. Mary was guiding him and preparing him for his First Communion. When this solemn and precious moment arrived, Alexander thought his heart was opening and Jesus taking possession of it in a sensible manner. The memory of this vision bound him so powerfully to the Tabernacle, that it was difficult to remove him from it, and every one in the town called him "the child of the high altar." Mary bestowed upon him truly maternal favors: while he studied she would turn the leaves of his book: in his illnesses she would cool the heat of his fever by surrounding him with flowers. Thus protected by Mary's loving presence, the pious student never shared in any worldly gayety, nor took part in any dangerous intercourse or any dissipating recreations.

It is thus that both childhood and adolescence, when placed under the surveillance of the Virgin of the Eucharist, and faithful to her cult, will be spent in a pure manner and will prepare faithful children for the Church, and citizens for heaven adorned with every virtue. (*Parterre de Notre-Dame de la Première Communion.*)

Practice—Let us pray for the exact accomplishment of the Decree of the Holy Father concerning the First Communion of little children, and for the catechists who prepare them.

Aspiration—Hail, O Mary who hast vanquished all heresies against the Holy Eucharist, through the apostolate of thy prayer!

TWENTY-FIFTH DAY

Mary's Apostolate

I. The soul that lives on the Eucharist ought to occupy itself, before everything else, with the interests of this Adorable Sacrament. Now the first and dearest of all these interests to Jesus is His priesthood. It is through the priest that the Blessed Sacrament is given to us. By priests, Jesus receives that sacramental life which He consecrates to the glory of His Father; by them, He is more glorified than by even the most devout of the Faithful. He has given them all His rights and all His power.

Pray, therefore, for the priesthood; beg that vocations to it may be multiplied; labor to obtain holy, zealous priests for the people. This was Mary's prayer, her apostolate of predilection. And now, she not only begs her Son for holy vocations, but she guards and protects them. The priest is Mary's privileged child.

It is she who trains him to piety in youth and shields his virtue; she it is who nourishes his fervor, who leads him by the hand to the foot of the altar and presents him to the Bishop, as once she offered Jesus in the

Temple. She encourages him in the thousand sacrifices of study, in his combats against fear of the priestly responsibility. The priest formed by Mary!—O good and holy priest, how well Jesus will receive thee!

II. Mary lives again in the priest, and through him she continues her mission for souls and for the glory of her Divine Son. The first Incarnation was made in Mary and by Mary. In her the Word was made Flesh. In the hands of the priest, and at his word, Jesus Christ becomes our Bread.

The dignity of Mother of God is incomparable. She is the Mother of the King, consequently the Mother of the Angels and of men. The priest is the father of Jesus Eucharistic, the spiritual king of souls: he is a god on earth, *terrenus Deus,* who has received all the riches of God—who opens and closes heaven.

Mary nurtured Jesus, cared for Him at every age. The priest causes Jesus to increase in the soul, cares for Him there, conserves Him, until He has, as it were, come to maturity in the soul and transformed it into Himself.

Mary, as Mother, has all the rights over her Divine Son that maternity gives. The priest, also, has direct power over the Person of Jesus Christ. Mary is powerful only through Jesus. The priest, also, is powerful only through the graces that Jesus puts into his hands. Jesus places Himself at his disposal in order to give him greater power of action.

But Mary, in certain respects, may envy the privilege of the priest. She carried the Word made Flesh for nine months in her womb, and that was the end. The priest's power is never exhausted; he incarnates Jesus Christ every day, for his consecrating power is inherent in his priesthood. He is in this power like unto the Father, who begets the Son without ever exhausting Himself; like the sun, which daily renews the gifts of its light and heat.

Mary brought forth the Savior in His mortal state, frail and destined for the Cross. The priest brings Him down upon the altar in His glorious and Risen State. True, this glory does not appear to our carnal eye, but the Angels see it; it is a Sun radiant in the sight of heaven, but veiled to earthly eyes.

III. The mission and the duties of the priest in regard to the Eucharist and in regard to souls are the same as those of Mary.

The priest is, first of all, an adorer and the guardian of the Blessed Sacrament. He is, above all, a man of prayer: *"Nos autem,"* said the Apostles, *"orationi et ministerio verbi instantes erimus."* "Let us give ourselves to prayer and preaching." He must unite himself to the prayer of the Victim which he prepares and offers to the Eternal

Father. He must begin at the foot of the altar his exterior apostolate.

Mary in the Cenacle! Behold the Divine Mother in this first duty. Her office there is that of an adorer. She adores by taking care of the Eucharistic worship. She repairs the glory of God outraged by sinners. She consoles Jesus for His unrequited love. To the Father, she offers Jesus; to Jesus, she shows her maternal heart; while to the Holy Spirit, she presents souls, His inheritance and His temples, in order that He may renew them and inspire them with His love.

Behold what the faithful priest—one who understands the favor of the Savior's love for him—owes to Jesus!

The second priestly function is to announce Jesus Christ to the people. Mary is here again his sweet supporter. She educated Jesus, and she revealed the mysteries of His life to the Apostles and the Evangelists. She spoke incessantly of Him and made Him loved by all around. She was the first zealatrix of Jesus.

Now, behold what the priest has to do: preach, make Jesus in the Blessed Sacrament known; spread His worship and His reign with untiring zeal. For this, he addresses himself to Mary, who loves priests with a love of predilection. She loves them in Jesus, her Son, whose ministers they are; she loves them for the glory of God and the salvation of souls, whose apostles they are.

The priest, then, has duties to fulfill toward this tender Mother. He ought to be second to none in the honor he renders her, the tender love that is due her. He should most zealously make her known and loved.

As for us, if we love the Eucharist, if we desire to have It served, preached, loved by all, let us incessantly beg of Jesus, through Mary, to give us holy priests, apostolic workers, faithful adorers. The glory of the Blessed Sacrament and the salvation of the world are at stake.

MARY'S TENDER PROTECTION OF A PRIEST

Two priests once passing through the country of the Albigenses, came to a church; and though the times were those of open persecution, and everything was to be feared from savage heretics, they wished to celebrate Holy Mass; being especially moved thereto by the thought that it was Saturday and that they should say Mass in honor of Mary. One of them had already begun to celebrate, when the Albigenses appeared. They tore him from the altar, and after a thousand outrages cut out his tongue and left him half dead. His companion carried him as well as he could to a neighboring monastery, where they were most charitably received. On the eve of the Epiphany the poor dumb priest, hearing the religious chanting, had a great desire to join in the singing; and he would have liked very much to celebrate Holy Mass. In his fervent desires he addressed himself to Mary, and this sweet Mother, holding his missing member in her hand, appeared before him saying: "My dear son, since you lost your tongue and suffered so much only because you wanted to say Mass for the honor of Jesus, and for my glory, I return it to you from Him." At that very instant the good priest was cured, and with sonorous voice intoned a hymn of thanksgiving to the praise of Jesus and of His merciful Mother. (Nicolao Laghi, *trat.* VI, *c.* xxiv.)

Practice—Pray constantly for vocations to the priesthood, and exercise towards the priests of Jesus the most devoted and respectful charity.

Aspiration—O Queen of the clergy! send workers into the Vineyard of thy Divine son.

TWENTY-SIXTH DAY

The Divine Spouse and King of the Heart

I. In her adoration, Mary aimed at honoring all the different states of Jesus, at exalting Him under His dearest titles, those which establish most perfectly His empire over men's hearts.

She adored Jesus in His capacity of Spouse of souls. Union is the end of love. Jesus in giving Himself substantially to us in the Eucharist, unites Himself to our soul as His cherished spouse. As such He gives us all His riches; He gives us His Name, His Heart, His whole Self, but He expects something in return. Jesus is a jealous God. The soul, His spouse, must live for Him alone. Woe to him that steals from Jesus the spouse of His Heart!

Now, Mary, like a good Mother, would have the nuptials of her Beloved Son celebrated in a worthy manner. As formerly at Cana she prevented the embarrassment of the bride and bridegroom, so does she adorn the faithful soul with her own virtues, in order that Jesus may find it less unworthy of Him. Oh, yes! the best preparation for

Communion is that which Mary makes. Is it not a mother's task to clothe her daughter for her wedding day? She is ready to despoil herself for the occasion. Who can describe the care that this good Mother takes of the spouses of her Eucharistic Son, above all in regard to all that concerns the purity of their hearts, so that they may please their well-beloved Spouse?

But Jesus is also the Spouse of the Church, whose fruitful virginity makes Him the Father of a new generation of God's children. Mary also adored Him, then, as Spouse of the Church, and she loved the latter as her daughter, indissolubly united to her very dear Son. Mary would willingly have given her life for the Church. She protected her, defended her by incessant prayer; she gladly watched over her progress and shared her dangers, suffering with her and for her. And though Mother of the Church, she was at the same time her daughter, and, like the most submissive of her children, she obeyed Peter and John and *all* priests. She honored the holy ceremonies; she adored Jesus through the Church; through her worship, her liturgical prayers, her priesthood, in company with her children. Oh, what a beautiful adoration was that which united Mary and the Faithful at the foot of the Most Blessed Sacrament! Heaven itself might well have been jealous of it, for Mary was in the Church as the sun among the stars! God had good cause to love the earth, and Jesus His Tabernacle, for it was the heaven of love!

II. Again, Mary adored Jesus as King, for the Holy Eucharist is the Savior's royalty. By It He reigns in hearts and over society. Truth to triumph over men must pass through the Eucharist, in order to catch some of Its sweetness and become persuasive and appealing. So long as a man has not communicated, he has only the faith of truth, he has not yet the real faith of love, the joyousness and the sweetness of faith. He has met Jesus on his way, he has conversed with Him without knowing Him well. The Eucharist alone will reveal to him in all His power and light Jesus Christ and all the secrets of the Faith. Jesus, then, is King of truth through the Eucharist.

So, too, of the other virtues. The Eucharist is necessary in order that they may flourish in the heart. Communion is necessary to refine, to soften, to beautify them in the love of Jesus. Jesus must give Himself to me in Holy Communion in order to subjugate me by His love and be able to say to me: "My child, give Me thy heart." In the Eucharist alone, the love of Jesus Christ is royally served, since It gives Him a palace, a court, adorers.

Mary, then, adored Jesus as her King; but

she adored Him no longer in His poor, fugitive royalty of Bethlehem or of Egypt, nor as her Crucified King on Calvary. She adored Him in His permanent royalty, on His throne of glory, all veiled though He is. There He is invulnerable to the darts of His enemies, invincible in His victory, glorious in the triumph of His love. Mary saw the fulfillment of the prophecy of the Angel: "He shall reign in the House of Jacob forever. And of His kingdom there shall be no end." She saw the Eucharistic thrones multiply daily; every city, every village becomes His court and offers Him a palace. She beheld all the virtues flourishing in the world by means of the Eucharist, virtues that are the royal crown of the God who inspires and fosters them.

Oh, what sighs, what prayers for the Eucharistic reign of Jesus issued from Mary's heart in the Cenacle! Even as she had prayed for it she saw, in the course of the ages, the Eucharist spreading and the love of Jesus triumphing everywhere. At last, Jesus will be loved, His Eucharist will find everywhere sympathetic hearts; Its fire will envelop the world and by so doing will completely renew it.

O Divine King! yes, reign as Sovereign over my heart and my life, as Thou didst over Thy Blessed Mother. May Thy truth be my ensign of honor; Thy virtues, my shield of defense; Thy love, my word of command; and Thy greater Eucharistic glory, the fruit of my victory!

This is the ardent prayer of my heart, which I offer Thee through Mary, the Queen of the Cenacle, and the Mother of adorers.

THE MERCIFUL QUEEN OF PURGATORY

The most powerful means of helping the poor suffering souls in Purgatory is to have the Holy Sacrifice of the Mass celebrated for them. But when one places the unlimited fruits of the Blood of Jesus in Mary's hands, that she may apply them for the relief of these dear suffering brethren, their deliverance is practically assured.

A certain good brother, and very devout religious, having died, appeared to one of his old comrades and told him that he was enduring the pains of purgatory; suffering, however, little from the pain of sense, but much from the privation of God. He begged him to ask the Prior to add a prayer at Holy Mass for his intention. They hastened to satisfy him by granting this request, and the Prior saw the dear brother's soul full of joy and ecstasy beneath Mary's mantle, as she carried her love's glorious conquest triumphantly to heaven. (Nicolao Laghi, *t.* III.)

Practice—We should pray constantly to Mary to extend the Eucharistic reign of Jesus Christ throughout the whole world.

Aspiration—O Immaculate Heart of Mary, nuptial couch upon which the Spouse finds His delights, inflame us with the love that consumes thee!

TWENTY-SEVENTH DAY

THE EUCHARIST THE CENTER OF MARY'S LIFE

I. Mary shared the Eucharistic life of Jesus. Love desires a life in common with the Beloved. At Bethlehem and at Nazareth, Mary had lived the same poor, hidden life of Jesus; in Egypt, she shared His persecuted life; throughout the little villages of Judea, she led His apostolic life. She had always shared His life of suffering, consequently with good reason she would live the Eucharistic life of her Divine Son, which is the crown of all the others.

Mary lived, by means of the Eucharist, a life altogether interior and hidden, silent, separated from the world, with Jesus for her only witness and confidant. Her life was spent in contemplating the Eucharist and in thanking her Sovereign Lord for It. So absorbed was she in this, that her heart was filled with sweetness, and she had but one desire, to love Him still more, to give herself to Him more and more completely. Mary's body, even, shared the joy and heavenly peace of that life; it became entirely spiritualized: *"Cor meum et caro mea exul-*

taverunt in Deum vivum"—"My heart and my flesh have rejoiced in God, my Savior."

II. This Eucharistic contemplation is more active than passive. It is the soul giving itself incessantly to God, under the ever new and ever livelier impression of His goodness, under the ever-increasing action of the flames of His love, which purifies it, detaches it from all earthly things, and unites it more intimately with the Well-Beloved.

Recollection is the first condition necessary for this heavenly contemplation. The soul, free from all external impressions, disengaged from all irregular affections, goes straight to God, as the needle points to the pole. The soul, recollected and fixed on Jesus, nourishes itself with His truth, His goodness, His love. Prolonged prayer costs little or nothing, because, freed from all things, it can follow its Savior whithersoever He goeth; nothing urging or calling it elsewhere, it can then study the profound mysteries on which it meditates. It sees things as they really are in Jesus Christ; recollection and contemplation strengthen its sight and render it reflective and penetrating.

III. How perfect must have been Mary's contemplation before the Most Blessed Sacrament, with the great light of her faith, the purity of her life, the perfect love of her heart! Assuredly, distraction, that fever of the mind and heart, came not to trouble the repose of her soul in her Well-Beloved. Her soul, more united to Jesus than to the body that enveloped it, drank in long draughts of the living waters of grace and of love. She forgot the world about her in order to remain alone with Jesus; for it is characteristic of love to isolate itself, to concentrate itself in unity in order to unite itself more closely to the beloved.

Let the adorer, united to Mary Adoratrix, apply himself with patience, with constancy, to the virtue of recollection, to the exercise of the contemplation of Jesus Christ; studying at first to know Him rather than to enjoy Him; for love comes of truth known, and the grace of enlightenment is of more value than the greatest grace of sweetness and consolation. Truth remains, but sentiment passes.

Oh, happy the soul which penetrates, as Mary did, the sublimity of this mystery of love, who desires it, who asks it without ceasing, who incessantly exercises itself in it! The kingdom of God is within it!

THE FIRST PROCESSION OF THE MOST BLESSED SACRAMENT AT LOURDES IN 1888

Since the National Pilgrimage of 1888, the great pilgrimages of Lourdes have presented a peculiar characteristic: it is a Eucharistic demonstration in which the Divine Sacrament causes Its glory and Its power to shine more strikingly. Of course

Jesus the Savior was never forgotten amidst the pious homage tendered by the crowds to His most holy Mother. It must also be remembered that if Mary worked miracles upon souls and bodies, it was always through the omnipotent virtue of her Son, whose Real Presence dominates the blessed Grotto—who is God the sole Author of all these wonders. But that year, as the *Journal de Lourdes* remarks: "It has pleased our good Mother to efface herself that her Divine Son might shine forth in the Eucharist."

The 21st of August, 1888, was for the National Pilgrimage a day of trial: there were few cures, and towards evening a terrible storm prevented the torch-light procession from taking place. At the sight of the saddened, though not discouraged, pilgrims an inspiration from Heaven had suddenly dawned in the heart of a pious ecclesiastic. Why should not the Blessed Sacrament receive a triumphant ovation? And as the God of the Eucharist was being carried among the sick, why should not the multitude address Him with the same acclamations, the same prayers which in the days of yore had obtained the miracles which occurred during the mortal life of the Savior? This plan was, of course, favorably accepted.

The next day, at four o'clock in the afternoon, Jesus Hostia was leaving the Basilica preceded and followed by a great number of the Faithful bearing tapers in their hands. After Benediction, given in the Grotto, the invocations began, with an animation, a stress, an enthusiasm quite indescribable. A spirit of Heaven-sent rapture descended upon the crowd. From all the pallets, from all the beds, from all the vehicles where human infirmity lay prone and suffering, something heartrending, supplicating, came forth; and as though by a unanimous impulse, the crowd called upon the Son of the Immaculate, as of yore did the paralytic and the blind man of Jericho, "Lord! if Thou wilt, Thou canst heal me!"

But now, behold! in front of the Grotto eight of the sick have arisen. How describe such things? When the *Magnificat* was intoned, triumphant, prodigious, no one could restrain his tears. And ever since, every year in the numberless processions that unwind themselves near the blessed Grotto, the same enthusiastic faith bursts forth; the same ardent prayer on the part of the Faithful, the same prodigies of merciful power on the part of Jesus Christ present in the Blessed Sacrament take place. It is Mary at Lourdes who has really prepared the Eucharistic triumph of her Son. (*Les Miracles historiques du Saint Sacrement, par le P. Eug. Couet.*)

Practice—Often pray to God for the perseverance of persons consecrated to Jesus in the cloister and in the world.

Aspiration—O Mary, like new-born babes, we ask of thee our spiritual milk, Jesus Eucharistic!

TWENTY-EIGHTH DAY

Mary's Life of Union with Jesus

I. Mary lived in the Eucharist. He who truly loves, thinks, desires, acts, rejoices or sorrows in the person loved; he is his natural center. Jesus said: "Where thy treasure is, there is thy heart": and to His Apostles: "Abide in Me. . . . Abide in My love . . . as I abide in My Father's love."

Mary lived, then, in the Divine Eucharist, the center of her love. All her thoughts, words, actions came forth from It as sunbeams issue from the sun. The Eucharist was the oracle that she consulted, the grace that she followed.

II. Jesus in the Sacrament lives the same life of love which consumed Him in the days of His mortal existence. In His Sacramental state, He continues to adore His Father by His profound annihilation. He is still the Mediator and Intercessor, before the Divine Goodness, for the salvation of men.

Mary united with Jesus in prayer, adding thereto the exercise and the merit of the virtues that our Lord in His glorified state can no longer actually practice. She responded to Jesus' state of humiliation in the

Sacrament, by virtue and acts of humility; to His condition of Victim, by her actual endurance of suffering; to His state of propitiation, by her voluntary acts of mortification. To honor the hidden life of Jesus, Mary effaced herself, aiming at being nothing more than a human appearance, as it were, whose whole being and substance are changed, transformed into Jesus Christ. She is poor, as Jesus is in the Sacrament, poorer, even, since she can experience the real privations of poverty. Like Jesus, she obeys and honors His Sacramental obedience by submitting to the least of the ministers of the Church. To imitate His obedience, so sweet, so simple and so prompt, she is happy to obey, eager to yield at the least sign. In a word, Mary realizes in herself the Eucharistic life of Jesus Christ.

Mary, moreover, renewed in the Eucharist all the mysteries of the Savior's mortal life, perpetuating and renewing her gratitude with ever-increasing fervor.

III. Such ought to be the life of the adorer if he wishes to live in the Eucharist. But to attain this life of union, he must free himself from the slavery of self-love, which seeks self only—even in God's service; which speaks to Jesus of self only, of its own personal affairs; which knows not how to converse with Jesus by speaking to Him of Himself, of the interests of His glory, of the desires of His Sacred Heart; which knows not how to remain, calm and tranquil at His feet, satisfied with Him, desiring nothing but Him. He must free himself from that state which has not the patience to listen to Jesus, and which makes us like mercenaries impatiently awaiting our wage, like commission agents eager to set out.

Jesus has very few adorers who consider themselves sufficiently recompensed and happy in remaining with Him, occupied in serving Him as do the Angels in heaven, as Mary did in the Cenacle. He sees at His feet only beggars, or the restless, who seek help. In a royal palace, however, they know their duties as courtiers, know how to wait attendance on the king, seeking only by their presence to honor his majesty. Alas! that is merely the reign of the senses, and counts for nought. At the Eucharistic court of Jesus, it is the interior reign of His love —and we are afraid of it, we flee from it, we wish to *act*. Jesus alone, does not suffice for us; we must have something besides Him!

Mary, though, never lost the Eucharistic presence of Jesus. She acted only when He wished it, considering herself well occupied when at His feet, sufficiently recompensed in possessing Him.

THE NUMEROUS MIRACLES AT LOURDES DURING THE PROCESSION OF THE MOST BLESSED SACRAMENT

Contemporaneous science has for a long time sought the secret of our cures in the waters of the piscinas. The temperature of the water, its composition, all has been brought forward. "How do we know," said one romancer, "that in certain circumstances a bath in ice water might not save a consumptive?" And so it happens that, by one of those seeming whims of Providence, the original plan of Lourdes seems abruptly modified; a new appeal makes itself felt.

It is not only in the piscina, where the patient is surrounded by a certain mystery—it is during the procession, in the full light of day, under the eyes of a thousand witnesses that the cures take place.

They wanted to keep our God a silent Prisoner, enclosed in the Tabernacle. Behold! He comes forth. He passes through the crowds, His divine rays more resplendent than gold and precious stones, dazzle our eyes, bring back life to those who are dying on their beds, leading them after Him triumphant and transformed, penetrate the crowds and warm hearts and souls frozen and benumbed for years. Miraculous cures, miraculous conversions! Who can enumerate them?

It is interesting to study these manifestations which have been spreading since the year 1888. With them, all that constitutes the real life of the pilgrimages is developed; the crowds are greater; the Communions are more frequent, for that is the hearth from which supernatural life draws nourishment.

It was in 1888 that for the first time we made statistics of the cures which occurred where the Blessed Sacrament passed. That year they reached a proportion of sixteen per cent—about a sixth; seven cures at processions to forty at the pools. A great number of cures remains unreported as to place and manner. Often a cure begins at the piscina and terminates at the procession; more rarely, a cure begins at the procession and is completed at the piscina. In a great number of cases where there had been no results at the piscina, the cure took place before the Blessed Sacrament instantly.

The first cure mentioned to us was that of Nina Klin, a young woman of twenty-two, just out of the Paris hospitals. A container holding twenty-five pints of sulphuric acid had been spilled over her and she had been deeply burned. The nerves of the leg had been compressed in the scar, and for ten months she had been unable to move at all. Every treatment had been tried in vain—massage, electricity—no results had been obtained. Nina Klin had come with the National Pilgrimage. She was twice immersed in the piscina, but felt no improvement. On the twenty-second of August she was lying on a mattress in front of the Grotto when the Blessed Sacrament passed beside her. She was suddenly lifted up by a violent impulsion, and jumping from her bed she broke through the litters that surrounded her and followed the procession with an assured step. (*From the report of Dr Boissarie read at the Eucharistic Congress at Lourdes in 1898. Cf. Nouveau Recueil de Miracles eucharistiques, par le P. Eug. Couet.*)

Practice—In union with Mary, let us live the life of Communion and thanksgiving by interior recollection.

Aspiration—O Heart of Mary, magnificent Throne of the Hidden God, be thou exalted to the heights of the heavens!

TWENTY-NINTH DAY

The Perfect Servant of the Blessed Sacrament

I. *"Ecce ancilla Domini!";* "Behold the handmaid of the Lord!" exclaimed the Blessed Virgin; and her whole life was passed serving Him in the most perfect manner. She is the perfect model of our Eucharistic service. Her service in the Cenacle sums up her whole life. There she renewed all its phases, all its graces; there her virtues acquired their supreme perfection which was to render them worthy of heaven and of the immense glory that awaited her. To attach himself to this last link of Mary's life is the grace of a servant of the Eucharist; to get inspiration from her virtues and her devotedness is his strength and his rule. The spirit of a servant of Jesus is thus defined; devoted love to the Blessed Sacrament in the spirit and virtues of the Blessed Virgin.

It is disinterested devotedness. He does not devote himself in order to be perfect or to be happy, to amass for himself a spiritual fortune, or to gain a beautiful paradise. No, he devotes himself through pure love. True devotedness longs for one thing only, and that is to give pleasure, and to fulfill its duty. Now, our Lord does not ask us to serve Him in the outside world, not even in souls; but He says to us: "To ascend My throne of love, I must have adorers. Without such, I cannot be solemnly exposed. You will remain with Me, you will be My adorers; you will be attached to My Person; you will exist for Me, as I shall live for you. You shall go so far as totally to renounce your own will, for I want it for Myself. Renounce your personal interests, I will assume them." A king desires to build up the fortune of his subjects, though he does not tell them what he is going to do. So the field that we have to cultivate is our Lord Himself, Him alone. He retains us for Himself and commits Himself to our care. And the reward of this devotedness? It is to live near the King, to please Him, to be His favorites. Ah, let us serve Him for His own glory and efface ourselves in everything!

This devotedness ought, then, to be the devotedness of pure love, pure Eucharistic love for Jesus in the Blessed Sacrament. This love should absorb all else. Jesus gives Himself entirely to us and He wishes us, in return, to give ourselves wholly to Him. But He brings with Him a feeling of joy and happiness which spreads over our whole life. What! to be associated with the Eucharist! to become one of the staff of Jesus Christ! what is there greater on earth or in heaven? Go, then, undertake this service with joy and gladness. Love flies; it loves the service of Jesus better than its own repose, its own gratification. When we do not love, we do not want to go too fast, we delay our steps. But, like Mary, let us fly to the service of adoration of Jesus in the Eucharist who is waiting for us.

II. The service of our Lord is, therefore, a duty for us as it was for Mary. You are called to serve *Him* and not yourself. You must guard against using words which indicate an incorrect understanding of this sublime service. You should not say, for instance: "I am going to perform my service." No, all employees talk that way. You should say rather: "I am going to the service of our Lord." There is a vast difference between the two expressions, and an even greater between the two ideas. A courtier knows that it is correct to say: "I am in the king's service"; very well, then, let us say: "I am in the service of our Lord." By these words, we efface self, we lose sight of self altogether, and we put our Lord first.

This service embraces several functions. There are those which directly regard His Person, such as the Mass, Adoration, the Office; there are others that refer to His household and to the good of His servants. But all are functions which pertain to the royal service of the Master. Our Lord's house requires varied attentions, different material employments; we are not pure spirits. But in all these labors, it is the King's glory that we must seek, it is for Him alone that we must work.

Devotedness to the glory of the Most Blessed Sacrament—what is this glory that we owe Him? It is to refer to Him all the good that we do, to keep nothing for self; not to reserve a little competency, as it were, on the side. Let us be true servants of the Blessed Sacrament, as Mary was; servants who have no longer any other interests, no longer any personality, who are entirely consumed in the service of Jesus.

What a beautiful title is this—the "handmaid," the servant of the Lord. It is the one that Mary preferred before all others. It is the only one that she ever gave herself. In taking that title of our Mother, we must accept with it all the duties and the virtues that the name implies. All are contained in the *Magnificat:* the Lord "hath regarded the humility"—the lowliness—"of His handmaid." Ah, if any one should be humble and devoted it is the servant of the Lord! How would it be for a servant to choose what service she should render her master;

to be sparing of her time, to reserve some for herself?

And all Mary's virtues—take them in their final character in the Cenacle: they are nothing more than acts of her adoration. Mary adores by each one of her virtues. Adoration is the sum total of her whole life.

Therefore, to serve Jesus in the Most Blessed Sacrament, after the example of our Lady of the Cenacle, and as she did—there is the life of the true servant. His motto is: "All for the service of Jesus-Eucharistic, in union with Mary!"

NUMEROUS MIRACLES AT THE PROCESSION OF THE MOST BLESSED SACRAMENT AT LOURDES

Since 1888 the proportion of cures which have taken place at the passing of the Blessed Sacrament has continually increased at Lourdes. They rose rapidly from one-sixth to one-fifth, one-quarter, one-third, and at last to one-half, which was exceeded in 1894 and in 1898. We find, in this last year, forty cures at the procession as against seventy-five at the piscinas. There were a few fluctuations in '91, '92, '95, but as an average during those ten years the cures at the processions increased to sixty per cent.

The sick, however, did not wait for our statistics, to notice these coincidences. They hasten to come and group themselves in the Esplanade of the Rosary. They prefer to come there during the pilgrimages to take part in the great Eucharistic manifestations, for they know that many cures will be incontestably proved during these ceremonies.

In 1889 we find some very interesting cures. Here is a young blind girl, Mary Louise Horeau, nineteen years old, who does not distinguish the day from the night. She has to be both led and fed. She had had recurrent Keratitis, deeply seated eye trouble, her eyes having lost their clearness. She has not been able to get near the Grotto, so she waits by the piscina, having begged her friend to notify her the moment our Lord comes near her. The Blessed Sacrament comes surrounded by the acclamations of the crowd. "Here He comes!" says the friend of the poor blind girl. The sick one falls upon her knees. "Lord," she cries, "if You will, You can cure me!—Lord, make me see!" Instantly a blinding light crosses her line of vision; she feels a very acute pain, and her eyes are opened. She distinguishes the Grotto, the kneeling crowd—and Jesus, radiant with glory, who has blessed her. Her sight is restored; she can see the finest, most delicate objects. We examine her eyes; they are limpid and perfectly clear. (*Dr Boissarie.*)

Practice—Let us consecrate ourselves to works of Eucharistic devotion in imitation of Mary, the handmaid of Jesus in the Cenacle.

Aspiration—O Mary, Mother of fair love, make us love Jesus in the Blessed Sacrament as thou didst love Him!

THIRTIETH DAY

Mary's Triumph

I. On the day of her glorious Assumption into heaven, Mary received the crown of all her graces. Truly we should rejoice, for, although our Mother has been taken from us, we have not lost her. We simply send her before us to prepare our place in heaven and to acquire for us certain rights over the Heart of God. We may now say to Him with great confidence: "Our misery is great, it is true, for this earth is but a desolate valley, but it sends Thee to-day its most perfect treasure—a marvel that it could not be expected to produce—Mary, Thy Mother! Look, then, upon us with eyes of mercy, for the sake of this blessed flower of our garden which we offer Thee; it is the purest and the most beautiful this earth ever produced."

The triumph of Mary is also the triumph of Jesus. He will find His Mother again; He will once more be her Son, because of her presence. Jesus loved His Mother so much, how was it that He could separate Himself from her? He did so through love of us, for having given her to us as **our**

Mother, it was but right that He should allow us to enjoy this ineffable gift. But the time has now come to recall that gift, and Jesus comes Himself to seek His Mother: *Innixa super dilectum suum.* Mary died of love; the longing to see her Son and to be re-united with Him snapped her thread of life. Jesus is now to accord her a grand triumph. What passed between Jesus and His Mother at the moment of their meeting? Well, we know the joy of a mother and a loving son on meeting after a long separation. And Jesus, who so desired to see His Mother once more—with what loving embraces He must have welcomed her!

II. Jesus Himself introduces His Mother to the glorified state; He owes her compensation. All her life Mary was poor and despised, but now the hour has come when she is to be crowned with glory and honor. She enters the heavenly Jerusalem in splendor such as was never seen before: she enters by a special gate, open for her alone; for it is not fitting that she should pass through the portal of the simple elect. If the twelve Apostles are the twelve gates of heaven, Mary is the royal entrance to that celestial country, the gate *par excellence*. O august and holy Gate! how good it is to pass through thee! Doubtless the practice of the Faith will give us sure entrance into heaven; but it will make our entrance there doubly certain if we confide ourselves to Mary's clemency, which desires only our salvation. Let us seek to enter heaven through this gate, and not count so much on our works and on our fulfillment of the law, for when we come to examine these we shall be forced to acknowledge them to be very imperfect.

Jesus leads His Mother by the hand, up to the very Throne of God: "Behold, O Father, her with whom Thou art associated by Thy choice of her as My Mother—to give Me My Humanity!" And the Father therewith crowns her with her three most beautiful titles: Queen, Mother, and Mediatrix. But in Mary's diadem there are three pearls that shine with an even more dazzling brightness—the pearls of her humility, of her poverty, and of her suffering.

III. Mary was the most humble of all creatures, consequently in heaven she is now the most glorious. If she is seated on the throne nearest to that of her Divine Son, it is because she approached nearer than any other to the perfection of His humility. In her earthly life she had been looked upon as one of Eve's sinful daughters—she who had never felt the taint of original sin! she had been regarded as ambitious—she who never said a word in self-justification!

No one was so poor as Mary, and never was poverty so meritorious, for she was the Mother of the King of heaven and earth.

In order to imitate the poverty of Jesus, she worked in Nazareth, begged in Egypt. What could have been more poverty stricken than the House of Loretto? Our Lord's Justice owed her compensation. Then, too, she inherits all the merits, all the graces of her Son; she has the free disposal of these. All the graces of salvation, both natural and spiritual, will be given us by Mary; she is rich with the riches of God Himself.

And if Divine Justice did not oppose the inclinations of her maternal heart, the very gates of hell would soon be closed. The demon has been forced to acknowledge that he is never sure of victory so long as he whom Mary protects retains a breath of life. She supplicates, importunes and snatches, as it were, from God the graces of mercy and pardon for the most hardened sinners.

Lastly, if happiness is in proportion to suffering, no one in heaven is so happy as Mary, for having never loved as much as she, no one could have suffered so much. It was God's Will that Mary should suffer a continual martyrdom. Simeon's prophecy poisoned all her joy. From the moment of its utterance, Mary substituted for Jesus while He was still too young to suffer publicly.

And at the foot of the Cross she is nearest to Jesus in order that she may suffer more. Because Jesus wished to have her nearest to

Him in heaven, He united her more than any other creature to His sufferings and humiliations while on earth.

In a word, God has crowned Mary with glory and honor as the Masterpiece of His love. He alone is greater than she: *"Solo tonante minor!"* But, in the midst of her glory, Mary never forgets that she is our Mother. She ascended to heaven before us to facilitate our entrance there and to conduct us thither. She herself will come for us at that supreme moment of our lives—the hour of our death—if we only summon her to our aid!

NUMEROUS MIRACLES AT THE PROCESSION OF THE MOST BLESSED SACRAMENT AT LOURDES

Most interesting cures took place at Lourdes in 1889. Mrs Facq, from Pont-à-Mousson, mother of ten children, forty-four years old, who had been paralyzed for five years: She was carried to the piscinas in a fainting condition—dying. Should they bathe her while in such a state? But there is no hope, the Sisters say, if the Blessed Virgin does not cure her! Eight of the Lady Helpers go to work. They undress the poor patient. She is immersed in the water. Once in, the hiccoughs begin; her lips grow livid. It is the agony, the end. The prayers for the dying are recited. At that moment the little bell announcing the approach of the Blessed Sacrament is heard. Quickly they carry the patient along the way of Its passage, under torrents of rain. The Lady Helpers fall on their knees around the patient and try to raise her head. Vain efforts, the head falls back and the eyes remain closed. At this moment the Blessed Sacrament arrives. All of a sudden the patient raises herself, her eyes open and become fixed on the ostensorium. She rises, she stands, she walks to meet the Blessed Sacrament. She falls on her knees at His feet. The ostensorium is placed upon her head. She rises at once, and bare-footed, in the mud, her face beaming with joy, she walks behind the dais and it is with great trouble that she is prevented from climbing thus as far as the Basilica, and it is only in front of the Pilgrim's Asylum that she can be stopped.

We could also recall the cure of young Guy, from Montpellier. He had been cared for in the hospital for a long time without results. He had a lifeless, paralyzed, atrophied arm, the discolored cuticle came off in patches. With his good hand he raised the splint which held his arm and touched the ostensorium. Immediately he felt a violent shock and heat, power and life returned instantly to the paralyzed member. He removed the apparatus to find himself absolutely cured.

Beside him was a twelve-year-old child who had never walked; affected with suppurative tubercular hip disease, he was lying in a groove. When the Blessed Sacrament passed before him, he seized the humeral veil with both hands and held back the priest who carried the ostensorium. In vain did they try to make him loose his hold. "No," said he, "I will not give in until I can get up cured!" And after struggling a few moments, he surely did rise before the wondering crowd which rushed after him and carried him triumphantly.

I have said that we had reached to sixty per cent for cures at the passing of the Blessed Sacrament; this proportion has been exceeded. This year (1898) the pilgrimage from Arras found that all its patients were cured during the procession. For ten or twelve years, the great rendezvous where the deepest homage has been paid to the Eucharist is Lourdes.

These manifestations which at first were limited to the National Pilgrimages, have been adopted by all the pilgrimages. They are loved by all peoples and form for the future a part of all great religious ceremonies. In the footsteps of our missionaries, with the devotion to our Lady of Lourdes, they have reached and penetrated the most remote places.

The story of the cures effected since 1888, along the line of the processions, makes one of the finest pages ever written on Eucharistic wonders. (*Dr Boissarie.*)

Practice—Let us help to prepare those who are in their last agony to receive Holy Communion. We should notify the priest in time, and arrange a proper reception for our Lord in the homes of the poor.

Aspiration—O Mary, give us Jesus Christ now, and at the hour of our death!

LAST DAY

Consecration to Our Lady of the Most Blessed Sacrament

I. At the close of this beautiful month which we have consecrated to thee, O Lady of the Most Blessed Sacrament, after having meditated upon thy greatness, admired the perfection of thy adoration and Eucharistic service in the Cenacle, it remains for us to give ourselves entirely to thee, in order that thou mayest guard and direct us in our vocation as adorers.

We confide, then, to thy maternal care, the direction of our vocation and the graces of the sublime duties that it imposes upon us.

Our vocation of adorers is a beautiful one, the most beautiful of all, since it keeps us forever in the service of the Adorable Person of Jesus Christ in His Divine Sacrament. It is a privilege, since it gives us the right to go directly to His Sacred Person without an intermediary.

Our vocation is sublime since we share the functions of the Angels, and—if I dare say it—even those of the Blessed Virgin herself, in the service of Jesus Christ. Consequently, for such a divine vocation, certain qualities are requisite, certain virtues, and at least ordinary piety. But alas! each one of us is forced to say: "I have nothing of all this; on the contrary, I have many defects, many bad habits; and I am made up of self-love. I have no humility at all, no sweetness, no spirit of mortification. I do not know how to pray nor how to make a meditation. I have nothing but a worn-out routine of piety, a few paltry ideas of virtue, niggardly and imperfect. Alas! my God! Thou who shouldst have at Thy service all that is greatest, most perfect and most holy, how hast Thou chosen me, poor, infirm creature, full of miseries, still covered with the scars left by my sins, all leprous from the old man who still lives in me?

How dare I accept this grace, to dwell with the Angels, to be in the same house with Thy Holy Mother—to remain in Thy holy presence?

O Mary, my celestial Queen and my divine Mother, I cannot accept the honor of becoming the happy servant of our Eucharistic Jesus, if thou dost not consent to form me for this service, to clothe me with thy virtues, thy merits; if thou dost not take me for thy child, O Queen and Mother of the servants of Jesus, you who live only for Jesus, who love us only in Jesus and for Jesus.

I entrust, then, to thy keeping, O good Mother, the grace and the development of my vocation. I give myself to thee; do thou give me to Jesus. Formed and presented by thee, O blessed Mother, Jesus, my sweet Master, will receive me willingly and love me in thee.

II. If my vocation is a beautiful one, its duties are great and divine. I should pass my life in adoration at the foot of the Throne of Love Incarnate, occupied before that Eucharistic Throne, even as in heaven the Angels and Saints are occupied—and will be eternally—praising His infinite bounty, blessing His boundless mercy, thanking Him for His love, devoting myself to His glory, immolating myself for sinners, and consuming myself for the extension of His reign on earth.

I should live always with Jesus Hostia, as the Blessed Virgin at Nazareth and in the Cenacle, as the Saints in glory. I ought never to leave Him, not even to serve my neighbor. My mission is that of Magdalen the contemplative, with the Queen of the Apostles, in the Cenacle, praying before the Tabernacle, converting the world by her prayer at the foot of the altar; that of St Teresa, of St Catherine of Sienna, and of all those holy souls who carry on an uninterrupted apostolate of prayer and immolation.

I should honor in a very special manner the interior and hidden life of Jesus in the Blessed Sacrament. I should live unknown to men, despised by the world, forgotten even by my very own—dead to all, in order to live more closely united with Jesus in God.

But how can I, by myself, fulfill duties so sublime? How dare I even approach Jesus to serve Him? Alas! by myself, I should be ashamed to draw near Him.

But, O my good Mother, since thou dost deign to become my teacher, thou wilt allow me to adore Jesus with thee, to bless Him with thy praises, entreat Him with thy prayers, serve Him with thy hands, love Him with thy heart, and glorify him with thy sanctity. I shall then be thy disciple, thy child, and, dare I say it?—another Mary serving Jesus.

I shall tell thee, simply and artlessly, my faults, O my good Mother! I shall make my ignorance known to thee, my meager knowledge, my small successes. I shall give thee the tiny flowers of virtue that I shall gather and thou wilt offer them to Jesus.

On this condition alone do I hope to become a true servant of the Most Blessed Sacrament!

My God, behold Thy humble servant! May it be done to me according to Thy merciful goodness and Thy most wondrous love!

Our Lady of the Most Blessed Sacrament, Mother and Model of Adorers, pray for us who have recourse to thee!

NOVENA

IN HONOR OF

OUR LADY OF THE MOST BLESSED SACRAMENT

First Day

THE TITLE OF OUR LADY OF THE MOST BLESSED SACRAMENT

O Sacrament Most Holy, O Sacrament Divine,
All praise and all thanksgiving be every moment Thine!

(100 days' Ind.)

Blessed be the holy and Immaculate Conception
Of the Blessed Virgin Mary, Mother of God!

(300 days' Ind.)

O Virgin Immaculate, Mother of Jesus and our tender Mother, we invoke thee under the title of our Lady of the Most Blessed Sacrament, because thou art the Mother of the Savior who lives in the Eucharist, and because it was from thee that He took the Flesh and the Blood with which

He there feeds us! We invoke thee under that title because, again, thou art the sovereign dispensatrix of all graces and, consequently, of those contained in the august Eucharist, also, because thou didst first fulfill the duties of the Eucharistic life, teaching us by thy example how to assist properly at the Holy Sacrifice of the Mass, how to communicate worthily, and how to visit frequently and piously the Most Blessed Sacrament.

V. Pray for us, O Virgin Immaculate, our Lady of the Most Blessed Sacrament.

R. That the Eucharistic Kingdom of Jesus Christ may come among us!

LET US PRAY

Lord Jesus Christ, our King and our God, who having become Man to make us sharers in Thy Divinity, art truly our Bread in the adorable Eucharist, grant, we beseech Thee, that in venerating so great a Mystery, we may be mindful of the most sweet Virgin Mary, of whom Thou didst will to be conceived by the operation of the Holy Ghost! Grant, also, that we may imitate the worship that she rendered while on earth to this most august Sacrament, so that we may behold Thy Eucharistic kingdom spread and flourish throughout the whole world! O Thou who livest and reignest forever and ever! Amen.

INDULGENCED PRAYERS

Our Lady of the Most Blessed Sacrament, pray for us!
(*Indulgence of 300 days.*)

O Virgin Mary, our Lady of the Most Blessed Sacrament, who art the glory of Christians, the joy of the Universal Church, and the hope of the world, pray for us! Stir up in all the Faithful devotion to the Most Holy Eucharist, that they may render themselves worthy to communicate every day. (*Indulgence of 300 days for every recital of this prayer.*)

Let us with Mary Immaculate adore, thank, supplicate, and console the most sacred and beloved Eucharistic Heart of Jesus! (*Indulgence of 200 days for each recital.—Pius X, Dec. 19, 1904.*)

Second Day

MARY AND THE HOLY MASS

O Sacrament Most Holy, etc.
Blessed be the holy, etc.

O Virgin Immaculate, after having been present at the death of thy Divine Son on Calvary, where thou didst unite thy immense sorrow to the Redeemer's sacrifice, thou didst frequently assist at the real, though mysterious, renewal of that adorable Sacrifice in the celebration of the Holy Mass. Teach us by thy example to esteem as it deserves the divine action performed at the altar, and obtain for us the grace to be able often, and even daily, to assist piously at the Holy Sacrifice.

Versicle, Response, and Prayer as on the first day.

Third Day

MARY AND HOLY COMMUNION

O Sacrament Most Holy, etc.
Blessed be the holy, etc.

O Virgin Immaculate, thy Communions were the most fervent, the most holy that ever were made! When thou didst possess thy Divine Son in thy breast, thou didst love Him with a love exceeding that of any other creature soever for his God. Teach us to make Holy Communion the center of our life, and may that life be spent in preparing us for so great an action and in thanking God for so inappreciable a benefit!

Versicle, Response, and Prayer as on the first day.

Fourth Day

MARY AND THE REAL PRESENCE

O Sacrament Most Holy, etc.
Blessed be the holy, etc.

O Virgin Immaculate, who, after the ascension of thy Divine Son, didst console thy exile on earth by the Real Presence of Jesus in the Sacrament, and didst spend before the tabernacle the greater part of thy days and even thy nights, make us comprehend the treasure we possess on the altar. Inspire us to visit often the God of Love in the Sacrament in which He abides to receive the homage that He deserves by so many titles, and to guide, protect, and console us in this exile!

Versicle, Response, and Prayer as on the first day.

FIFTH DAY

MARY, THE MODEL OF ADORERS

O Sacrament Most Holy, etc.
Blessed be the holy, etc.

O Virgin Immaculate, thou art our perfect Model in the service of the Divine Eucharist. With the most lively faith and the most profound respect thou didst adore Jesus hidden under the sacramental veils. After thy example, we desire to render to the Sacred Host all the honor due the Divinity and the glorified Humanity of the Son of God made Man. We wish to maintain at all times in the holy place the modesty and recollection becoming true adorers.

Versicle, Response, and Prayer as on the first day.

Sixth Day

MARY, THE MODEL OF THANKSGIVING

O Sacrament Most Holy, etc.
Blessed be the holy, etc.

O Virgin Immaculate, who didst return to Jesus so perfect thanksgiving for the institution of the Divine Eucharist and the ineffable Gift in which the Savior exhausted His power and the treasures of His Heart, teach us to thank thy Divine Son for this great benefit, and especially to make our thanksgiving well when we have had the happiness of receiving Him in Holy Communion.

Versicle, Response, and Prayer as on the first day.

Seventh Day

MARY, THE MODEL OF REPARATION

O Sacrament Most Holy, etc.
Blessed be the holy, etc.

O Virgin Immaculate, thou didst adore thy Divine Son in His state of perpetual Victim, always immolated on our altars, incessantly demanding, by His death, grace and mercy for sinners. We unite with thy dolors and thy perfect reparation. We desire to accept our daily trials for love of Him, and with thee to console Jesus for the ingratitude of men and the outrages He daily receives in the Blessed Sacrament.

Versicle, Response, and Prayer as on the first day.

Eighth Day

MARY, THE MODEL OF PRAYER

O Sacrament Most Holy, etc.
Blessed be the holy, etc.

O Virgin Immaculate, while the Apostles went to preach the Gospel, thou didst remain close to the tabernacle, supplicating for them the goodness of the Savior, and thy prayer obtained for them the grace to convert the world! Teach us to pray, above all, to pray near the tabernacle, where Jesus wills to abide continually in order to hear our petitions. Teach us to pray for the extension of the Eucharistic kingdom, for the salvation of the whole world, for the exaltation of the Holy Church, and most especially for the sanctification of the clergy and the conversion of sinners.

Versicle, Response, and Prayer as on the first day.

Ninth Day

MARY, THE DISPENSATRIX OF EUCHARISTIC GRACES

O Sacrament Most Holy, etc.
Blessed be the holy, etc.

O Virgin Immaculate, Mother most loving, and admirable Model of adorers of Jesus in the Blessed Sacrament, thou art also the dispensatrix of the graces necessary to fulfill that great duty! Grant us, then, we beseech thee, as the fruit of this novena, the virtues that will render our adoration less unworthy of thy Divine Son. Teach us to honor so well this Mystery of mysteries that we may receive here below the graces It contains, in order to enjoy in heaven the eternal life of which It is the pledge!

Versicle, Response, and Prayer as on the first day.

LITANY OF THE BLESSED VIRGIN

Lord, have mercy on us.
Christ, have mercy on us.
Lord, have mercy on us.
Christ, hear us.
Christ, graciously hear us.
God the Father of heaven, have mercy on us.
God the Son, Redeemer of the world, have mercy on us.
God the Holy Ghost, have mercy on us.
Holy Trinity, one God, have mercy on us.
Holy Mary, pray for us.
Holy Mother of God,
Holy Virgin of virgins,
Mother of Christ,
Mother of divine grace,
Mother most pure,
Mother most chaste,
Mother inviolate,
Mother undefiled,
Mother most amiable,
Mother most admirable,
Mother of good counsel,
Mother of our Creator,
Mother of our Redeemer,
Virgin most prudent,
Virgin most venerable,

} Pray for us.

LITANY

Virgin most renowned,
Virgin most powerful,
Virgin most merciful,
Virgin most faithful,
Mirror of justice,
Seat of Wisdom,
Cause of our joy,
Spiritual vessel,
Vessel of honor,
Singular vessel of devotion,
Mystical rose,
Tower of David,
Tower of ivory,
House of gold,
Ark of the covenant,
Gate of heaven,
Morning star,
Health of the sick,
Refuge of sinners,
Comforter of the afflicted,
Help of Christians,
Queen of Angels,
Queen of Patriarchs,
Queen of Prophets,
Queen of Apostles,
Queen of Martyrs,
Queen of Confessors,
Queen of Virgins,
Queen of all saints,
Queen conceived without original sin,
Queen of the most holy Rosary,
Queen of Peace,

} Pray for us.

Lamb of God, Who takest away the sins of the world, spare us, O Lord.

Lamb of God, Who takest away the sins of the world, graciously hear us, O Lord.

Lamb of God, Who takest away the sins of the world, have mercy on us.

It is not necessary to add any versicle, response or prayer in order to gain the 300 days' indulgence attached to every recital of this Litany of the Blessed Virgin Mary.